White Water Massif Central

Fluffy's guide to the friendly rivers of Southern France.

Peter Knowles

Rivers Publishing U.K.

Photographs are as credited, with others by the author.

Front cover: River Orb, looking upstream to Vieussan.

Back cover: Charlotte and Fluffy (photo Peter Knowles), Upper Allier - 'le Deculottoir' rapid and Jonchères castle. The beach at Roquebrun on the Orb.

Cover Design by Leon Reichel.

Drawings and cartoons are by Alan Fox (Foxy), Ben Ramsden, and local artists.

Maps were drawn by Peter Knowles & Fiona Jackson.

ISBN: 0-9519413-6-4.

A CIP catalogue record for this book is available from the British Library.

Printed by Cambrian Printers, Aberystwyth, Wales.

Trade enquiries:

- **U.K. and Europe**: to Cordee Outdoor Books & Maps,
  3a De Montford St, Leicester LE1 7HD, UK, Fax: 0116 247 1176.
- **Other countries**: to Rivers Publishing U.K.
  125 Hook Rise South, Surbiton, Surrey KT6 7NA, UK, Fax: +44 208 391 5114.

Disclaimer

The information and advice given in this book were written in good faith, but the reader is warned that nothing in this book should be regarded as 100% accurate: this book was written by humans so there are bound to be errors, rivers and rapids change, and some information is out of date before it is printed. All advice and information should be treated with caution and checked locally. The publishers, authors and contributors can accept no responsibility for any loss, injury, or inconvenience sustained by any person as a result of information or advice contained in this guide.

A typographic error in the guidebook had forced Henry into a difficult situation ...

WARNING Printed using Laser-phobic ink

This may degrade if scanned by photocopiers or similar devices.

Fluffy and the author share a rest from the hardships of river research.

The Author

Peter Knowles first paddled the rivers of the Massif Central with the Canoe Camping Club in 1968 and then for many seasons worked for PGL Adventure as river leader and instructor on the Ardèche.

He has always liked canoe camping, and white water added the buzz of excitement, so he persisted in learning to roll - taking some four years - just in time for one of the first kayak trips down the Grand Canyon of the Colorado in 1973. Since then he has led many expeditions and run 'quite a lot of rivers' in many different countries and continents, including more than a few first descents. In 1983 he led his first trip to Nepal and since then has been exploring and running the rivers of the Himalaya - he was selected as one of 20 'modern explorers' in an exhibition at Britain's Royal Geographical Society. More recent adventures include trips to Ecuador, Iran; first descents, and filming for American television in Mexico and Bhutan.

He wrote the first edition of White Water Nepal in 1992 and then became a specialist publisher. He now tries to stay warm and dry sitting in front of a word processor, writing about rivers. Friends keep trying to drag him off to some exotic river to get cold, wet and scared yet again - so the research and writing of White Water Massif Central seemed like a perfect excuse!

Acknowledgements

This book is the product of many people's input, ideas and help and I should like to say a big thank you to all the many paddlers who have shared their time and experience.

Most of the river research for this volume was done by friends and myself over the summers of 2000 and 2001, mainly paddling a Mad River 'Teton' and Dagger 'Legend' canoes - both of which were excellent choices -'Fluffy' stayed dry for most of the time. I spent two wonderful summers paddling the rivers of the Massif Central - researching and writing this book has re-confirmed my basic love for the delights of canoe touring.

Subsequently many paddlers (both in the UK and France) helped by checking the river write-ups, whilst others supplied articles, photos, drawings, information and ideas. I think this all illustrates that international canoeists are a genuinely nice fraternity! Throughout this book you will see that we have used the 'Royal we' as an acknowledgement that this is the work of so many.

I would like to say a special thanks to Sue Richardson, the Banks family - Mark, Kate, Thomas, William and Charlotte, Norman and Pam Taylor, Peter and Lesley Taylor, and Graham Murphy, who have been widely involved and helped on many aspects of this book.

We do our best, but no guide book is ever really finished or perfect - if you do spot a mistake or something that could be improved then please write and tell us - we publish any important updates on our website. I hope you enjoy this book and have some wonderful journeys on the rivers of the Massif Central.

Good Paddling! Peter Knowles www.riverspublishing.co.uk

Many thanks to:

Mark, Kate, Thomas, William and Charlotte Banks
Graham Bland
Monsur Darlington
Ian Days
Philippe Durand
Alan Fox
Mike Gallagher
Ray Goodwin
Dave Hallewell
Fiona Jackson
Robin Knapp
Michel Lagaume
Philippe Lariviere
Gus MacDonald
Dawn Macrae
Dave Manby
Jeremy Murland
Graham Murphy
Chris Nichol
Alain Nicolet
Hannah Paul
Jack Pease
Claude Peschier
Ben Ramsden
Patrice de Ravel
Sue Richardson
Carolyn Steane
Lester Stuart
Norman and Pam Taylor
Peter and Lesley Taylor
Rob Taylor
Peter Thorn
Claude Weisman
Safaraid
PGL
Dagger
Mad River Canoes

Allier - looking downstream from the bridge at Lavoûte Chilhac.

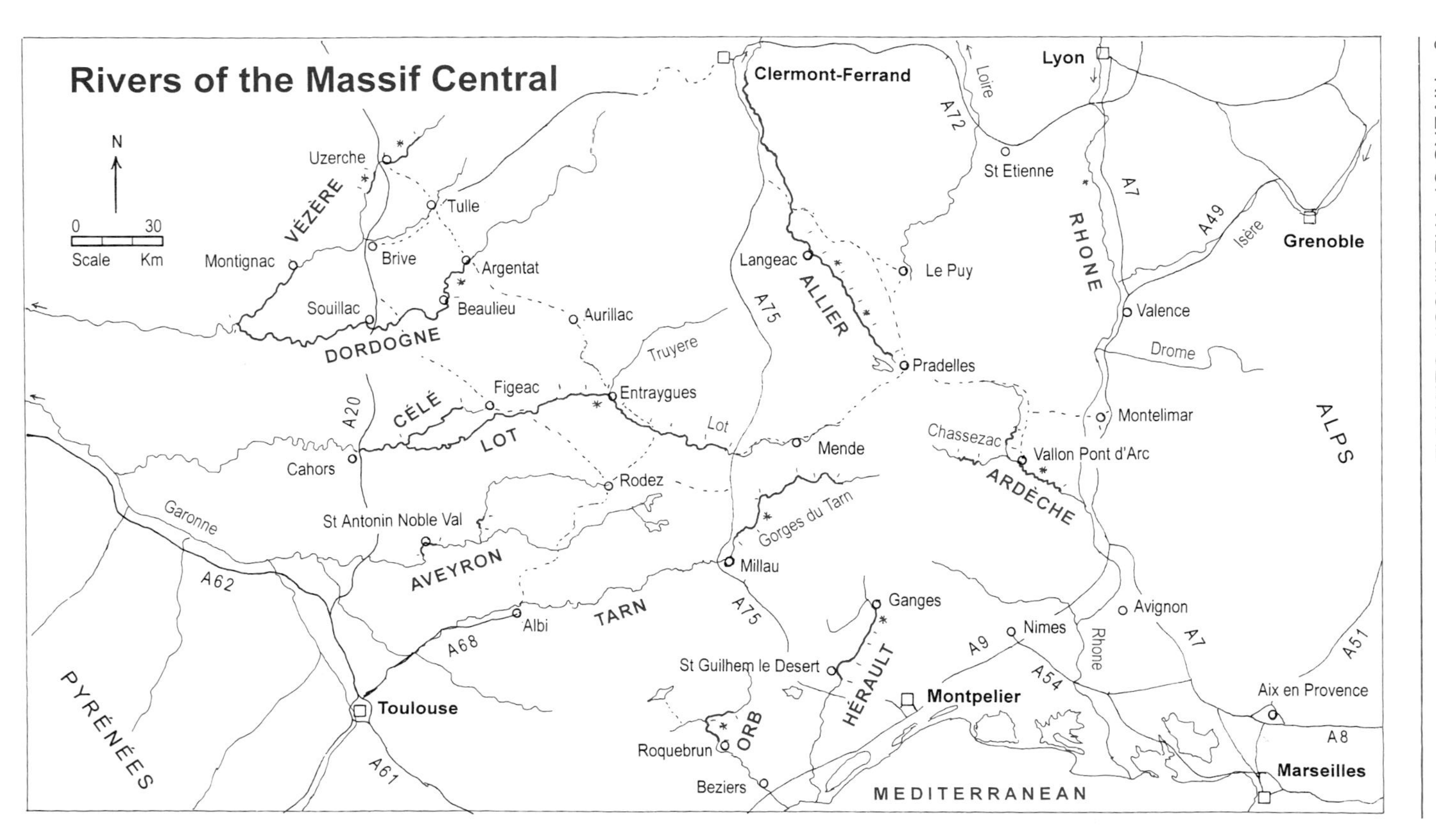
Rivers of the Massif Central
N
0 30
Scale Km
Uzerche
VÉZÈRE
Tulle
Montignac
Brive
Argentat
Souillac
Beaulieu
DORDOGNE
Aurillac
Truyere
Figeac
Entraygues
CÉLÉ
A20
LOT
Lot
Cahors
Rodez
Garonne
St Antonin Noble Val
AVEYRON
A62
Albi
TARN
A68
PYRÉNÉES
Toulouse
A61
Clermont-Ferrand
Langeac
ALLIER
A75
Le Puy
Pradelles
Mende
Gorges du Tarn
Millau
St Guilhem le Desert
HÉRAULT
Ganges
ORB
Roquebrun
Beziers
MEDITERRANEAN
Montpelier
A9
Nimes
A54
Rhone
Avignon
A7
A51
Aix en Provence
A8
Marseilles
Lyon
Loire
A72
St Etienne
RHONE
A49
Isère
Grenoble
Valence
Drome
Montelimar
Chassezac
Vallon Pont d'Arc
ARDÈCHE
ALPS

Allier

River and run	Class	Km	Stars	Scen.	Fluffy	Busy	Notes
St Etienne >	3 (5)	16	★★★	✿✿✿	-	<10	Technical, fun kayaking, very pretty.
Chapeauroux >	2 (3)	18	★★★	✿✿✿	☺	<50	'Jewel of a run' for canoes, fine gorge
Monistrol >	3-(3+)	10	★★	✿✿	-	<50	Good play boating and rafting run.
Prades >	2+	15	★★	✿✿	☺	<50	Pretty, scenic, friendly, canoe run. .
Langeac >	1-2	17	★★	✿✿	☺☺	<200	Old villages, granite cliffs, green river
Lavoûte Chilhac >	1-2	21	★★	✿✿	☺☺	<50	More of the same.
Brioude to Cournon	1(2)	67	★	✿	☺	<10	Pastoral & ideal canoe-camping.

Ardèche

River and run	Class	Km	Stars	Scen.	Fluffy	Busy	Notes
Chassezac Gorges	1-2(2+)	8	★★	✿✿✿	☺☺	<50	Technical paddling, splendid gorge.
Ardèche les Défilés	1-2	18	★	✿✿	☺	<200	Tamer version of the Gorges below
Ardèche - Pont d'Arc	2 (3-)	6	★★	✿✿✿	☺	>200	Foretaste of the Gorges below
Gorges de l'Ardèche	2 (3)	26	★★★	✿✿✿	☺	>200	A world Classic !

Hérault

River and run	Class	Km	Stars	Scen.	Fluffy	Busy	Notes
Ganges to Aubanel	2 (3-)	13	★★	✿✿	☺☺	<200	small river, diverse scenic run.
Moulin de Bertrand >	2	11	★	✿✿	☺	<50	a wild green canyon.
St Guilhem >	4	5	★★	✿✿	-	<10	convoluted run for deviant kayakers

Orb

River and run	Class	Km	Stars	Scen.	Fluffy	Busy	Notes
Poujol to Tarassac	2+	10	★★★	✿✿	-	<50	Fine rapids and a wild valley.
Tarassc to Roquebrun	2(2+)	15	★★★	✿✿✿	☺	<200	'Gorges de l'Orb' - superb canoeing.

Tarn

River and run	Class	Km	Stars	Scen.	Fluffy	Busy	Notes
le Pont du Tarn >	2-3	18	★★	✿✿	-	<10	*Usually insufficient water in Jul-Aug.*
Montbrun >	1-2	10	★	✿✿	☺☺	<50	Scenic introduction
Sainte Enimie >	1-2	14	★★	✿✿✿	☺☺	<200	Old villages & deep gorges
la Malene to Ps de sc	1	10	★★★	✿✿✿	☺☺	>200	Spectacular and popular run.
les Vignes to le Rozier	1-2(3)	10	★★★	✿✿✿	☺	<200	Wild water and wilder scenery
le Rozier to la Cresse	1-2(2+)	10	★	✿✿	☺	<200	Valley now wider.

Aveyron

River and run	Class	Km	Stars	Scen.	Fluffy	Busy	Notes
Gorges du Najac	2 (3-)	5	★	❁	☺	<50	Short fun run.
St Antonin to Cazals	1-2	8	★	❁❁	☺	<50	Scenic run with good beaches.

Lot

River and run	Class	Km	Stars	Scen.	Fluffy	Busy	Notes
St Laurent >	3	11	★★★	❁❁	-	<10	*Usually insufficient water in Jul-Aug.*
Pomayrols to St Gn.	2+	5	★★	❁❁	☺	<50	Tight gorge & fun playboating spot.
Barrage >	2-3	11	★★	❁	☺	<10	*Usually insufficient water in Jul-Aug.*
Espalion to Estaing	1-2	14	★	❁	☺	<10	*Usually insufficient water in Jul-Aug.*
Barrage to Hydro plant	3(4+)	3	★★	❁	-	<10	*Usually insufficient water in Jul-Aug.*
Hydro plant >	2-3	5	★★	❁❁	-	<10	*Usually insufficient water in Jul-Aug.*
Entraygues >	2(3-)	10	★★	❁❁	☺	<50	Classic run.
le Port >	1 (2)	11	★★	❁❁	☺☺	<50	Friendly, ideal beginners run.
Grand Vabre >	1	12	★	❁❁	☺	<10	2 weirs
Livinhac to Cahors	1	106	★	❁❁	-	<10	Scenic canoe touring but many weirs

Célé

River and run	Class	Km	Stars	Scen.	Fluffy	Busy	Notes
Boussac to Bouzies	1 (2)	48	★	❁❁	☺☺	<50	Friendly, small, ideal family run.

Dordogne

River and run	Class	Km	Stars	Scen.	Fluffy	Busy	Notes
Argentat to Beaulieu	2(2+)	25	★★	❁❁	☺	<50	Fast wide river, a sporty run.
Beaulieu to Souillac	1 (2)	55	★★	❁❁	☺☺	<200	A Classic canoe touring stretch.
Souillac to Beynac	1	44	★	❁❁	☺☺	>200	Famous villages, popular tourist run
Beynac to Mauzac	1	44	★	❁	☺	<50	Quiet, mellow run.

Vézère

River and run	Class	Km	Stars	Scen.	Fluffy	Busy	Notes
Peyrissac to Uzerche	2	17	★★	❁❁	☺	<10	Delightful, small, unspoilt river.
Vigeois to Estivaux	3	12	★★★	❁❁	-	<10	Granite gorge - a fun kayak run.
Montignac to Limeuil	1	47	★	❁❁	☺	<200	Famous pre-historic caves.

Notes

★ **Stars** for paddling are 1-3, a subjective measure of satisfaction at that grade.

❁ **Scenery** - our subjective measure from 1-3.

☺ **Fluffy's** rating 1-2 - an idea of how friendly we think the river is for **children**.

Busy is how many boats you might **expect to meet** on a typical day in high season.

Dordogne - shooting the glissiére at Beaulieu

Introduction

Why the Massif Central ?

The Massif Central is the upland area in the heart of France - not an area of high mountains like the Alps but an area of rolling hill and sweeping plateaux. This book is a guide to the rivers running off this upland - these rivers don't have the gradient or the power of Alpine rivers so they offer easier and friendlier paddling - ideal for families, canoe camping, or as a warm-up to kayaking in the Pyrénées or the Alps.

The northern part of these uplands is predominantly volcanic in origin, so the rivers tend to be steep-sided valleys with basalt cliffs in places. In the south the rock is limestone, and the rivers have cut spectacular and famous gorges through these limestone plateaux - the Gorges de l'Ardèche and the Gorges du Tarn are perhaps the most famous.

Because it's a guide to the rivers this guide covers more than just the upland area, but takes us down into the historic river valleys at the heart of France - the land of ancient fortresses, beautiful châteax, and timeless villages - famous areas like the Dordogne valley, and World Heritage sites such as Conques or St Guilhem le Désert.

In historic times the rivers in this book were at the heart of French life, they provided water for washing, drinking, fish and wildlife for food, power, and most importantly of all transport. Long before roads and the recreational canoeist, these rivers, like the Dordogne, Ardeche, and Lot were all the main means of transport with goods and people being carried in small flat-bottomed wooden barges. Travel down these rivers today and you are paddling through a real-life history and geography lesson - also a gastronomic one if you so choose - because many of these valleys are famous for the quality of their food and wine!

River tourism in the Central Massif goes back some 150 years to when 'les Bateliers' took the first tourists through the Gorges de l'Ardèche and it is now recognised as an important, and ecologically friendly source of tourist revenue (Estimates of the tourism benefits of rafting, kayaking and canoeing suggest that these are probably worth over 100 million euros per year in indirect revenue for Europe as a whole). It is sad to contrast this to the current situation in most areas of England and Wales where medieval property laws mean that rivers are not shared for recreation and local communities lose the economic benefits from this type of tourism.

Our message is to come to the Massif Central, run these wonderful rivers and spend your money in local communities: you will be made welcome, and you will be helping to protect the rivers that you enjoy. Note that throughout France (as in most of Europe) you are welcome as a tourist to run the rivers without permit, payment or licence - you are merely asked to follow any local regulations, to behave considerately, and to follow the country code.

Using this guide

Which rivers are included?

This guidebook hopefully includes every river in the Massif Central which is class 2 or above and **has sufficient water level in the peak summer months**. We have included a few important, classic rivers that are just class 1 (for example the Dordogne), but have missed out lots of flat rivers with weirs on because Fluffy doesn't like rivers like this!

Local French paddlers all say things like "Why haven't you included the 'so and so' river - it's an absolute dream - a brilliant paddle in the spring", etc. - but if there is the likelihood of no water in the summer, then sorry, but all it gets is a mention.

This is a guidebook primarily for those people paddling class 1-3 and the accent is very much on open canoeing rather than kayaking, however for the more experienced paddler, we hope it gives an overview and opens the doors to the other more difficult rivers of the Massif Central that are covered in French guidebooks..

The rivers in this guide are listed in a **clockwise order**, starting with the Allier.

River descriptions

We have tried in this book to give a 'feel' for each run and the important things that most paddlers would probably want to know if they were thinking of running it. What these river descriptions are not is a blow by blow account of how to run each rapid - this would take the fun out of paddling! We have normally noted major rapids, bridges, weirs or hazards, but be warned - rapids sometimes get washed away and new ones appear.

1. The **stars** for paddling are 1-3 and our measure of subjective overall satisfaction at that grade.
2. We have tried to do the same for **scenery**.
3. **Fluffy's** rating is an idea of how friendly we think the river is for children.
4. **Water quality** is poor, ok, good, or excellent. (poor you would not want to swim in it, excellent you wouldn't mind drinking it?). This is our subjective opinion taking a broad view. Government bodies test the water on a regular basis at popular bathing beaches but these are only at a few spots on the river so not necessarily representative. (see www.sante.gov.fr/htm/dossiers/baign.)
5. **Water temperature** is warm or cool - happily we didn't find any cold rivers!
6. **Busy** is how many boats you might **expect to meet** on a typical day in high season - <10, <50, <200 or >200. This is different and much less than the total number of boats per day which may exceptionally be in the thousands.
7. **Water volume** - on most rivers, we have tried to give an idea of water volume, as an estimated figure in cubic metres per second ('cumecs'). This is the typical low water volume in say early August.
8. **Distance** is in kilometres measured down the middle of the river (some paddlers we know will do twice this distance!) We have deliberately not tried to give any time estimates as this varies so much between different people.

How difficult?

Note that the **class of difficulty is for low flows** in the middle of the summer - with a higher volume the difficulty will normally increase and the river can become dangerous.

We have used the standard International Classification of Difficulty (see Appendix A) when grading these runs, and like many other modern guide books we have used + and - grades and ( )s. We think that these two ideas make the classification scheme a lot, lot, more meaningful.

Where we call a run **class 2** we mean that in our opinion this is the overall standard - there may be long sections of lower difficulty, but to do the run safely you need to be 100% capable of paddling at this level.

Class 2 (3) means that in our opinion the overall standard of the run is Class 2, but there are a few (normally one or two) class 3 rapids that can usually be easily portaged if required.

We have based our opinion on the class of difficulty of the river as it was when we, or our informants, ran it. Landslides, roadworks, floods, etc. may completely change a river and make it easier or harder - it's always sensible to seek up-to-date advice from other paddlers or canoe hire companies.

Class 2 rapid on the Allier below Chapeauroux *Kate Banks*

Safety

This is a 'Where to go' book rather than a 'How to do it' book - if you have never paddled before we recommend you take some lessons with a canoe school, or qualified instructor. That being said, without prejudice, the following advice, for adults, may be helpful.

- Most sensible beginners should be happy paddling on class 1 or even class 1-2. (Hire companies certainly don't insist on any previous experience for rivers like the middle Dordogne). For class 2 or 2+ you should have some previous experience and/or make your journey as part of a guided group.
- It is almost unknown for anyone to drown on class 1, 2 or 3 water when wearing a properly-secured buoyancy aid.
- If you have doubts about your ability to paddle a run, then pay a little extra to join a guided group (for the inexperienced the hardest thing is working out where to run a rapid).
- Most of the rivers in this book have a low flow and are shallow in the summer months so that if you do capsize, it will probably be completely harmless - the main danger is injury from being hit by your boat, rocks, and/or other boats. If you are in a rocky rapid and there is a risk of the boat becoming pinned on the rocks then immediately exit and swim or wade away from your canoe. Alternatively if there is no risk of the boat pinning then hold on the upstream end of your canoe and swim it to the shore.
- If your boat does become pinned on a rapid, then salvage your canoe a few minutes later from the shore when the incident has stabilised and you have had time to assess the situation. If your boat is stuck hard on a rock, then ask for expert advice - it is easy to make the situation worse or injure yourself if you don't know what you are doing!

Children

If you intend to take your family canoeing then obviously you have a duty of care, need to be super careful, and build up suitable experience. So much depends on the experience and qualities of you and your children that it is difficult to make firm recommendations. For example, if you have only limited experience and decide to take your four old daughter down the Gorges de l'Ardèche - class 2(3) - then most people would consider you foolhardy. To take a four year old down the Célé - a small, friendly, class 1 (2) river in normal low water summer conditions, would be quite different.

On some rivers and sections there are regulations or guidelines on the minimum age of children (for the Gorges de l'Ardèche it is 7). Local canoe centres and hire companies will normally be able to advise you on this.

Don't be misled by the photos in this book of Charlotte, William and Thomas, (the original 'Outdoor Monsters') who have been steeped in outdoor experience and have survival skills honed from a very early age. Of course they had Fluffy to look after them as well as some fully certified adults!

Floods

Most of the rivers in this book are dam controlled and on the majority, the flow is maintained at a fairly constant level. On some there may be bigger changes due to power demands, but usually nothing to worry about unduly. In exceptionally rare circumstances, every couple of years or so, there may be a flood, often in late summer after unsettled weather with thunder storms in the hills.

If the river rises suddenly whilst you are on it - then this may be because of a flash flood in the hills so do not be tempted to continue - stop immediately, pull your boat up at least 2m above the river level, and watch and wait to see to see how the situation develops and if the river goes down again. If necessary tie your boat up and evacuate by land. See the Ardèche floods article.

Note that there is an excellent system of flood warnings in place throughout France so you should normally get told of any risk several hours beforehand, by for example your campsite patron.

River regulations

Most of the rivers in this book have regulations to protect the river and the environment. These are normally posted at the access points and available from Tourist Information Offices and Canoe Centres. Usually they include common courtesies like taking your litter home with you. On some rivers paddling times are limited from say 1000 to 1800 hours so that the anglers can have the river to themselves for the best fishing times early morning and evening .

Ardèche Floods

The Gorges de l'Ardèche are notorious for some extreme floods - where the affect of a normal flood has been magnified because the waters have been constrained by the narrow gorges. The largest recorded flood was in 1890 when the river rose **21 metres** above normal levels at Pont d'Arc and the river reverted to flowing where it used to in pre-history, along the line of the road. There is an ancient photo of this that you can see in the book 'Eaux Vives d'Ardèche'.

Major floods seem to happen every 5 years or so - we were caught in one in 1976 at Chataignerie Campsite (as it then was) and I can remember being one of four river guides desperately trying to pull the canoes up the beach, but to our amazement the water was rising so rapidly that we just couldn't do it fast enough and we lost about 20 canoes (half the fleet) to the flood waters which rose over 3 metres in an hour. Meanwhile that campsite, and every riverside one in the area had been evacuated under a well established programme and system of flood warnings. April and September seem to be the worst months - a flood in September 1997 is well remembered by the canoe hire companies because some 500 canoes were washed down the river - some as far as the Rhone!

So do take heed of any flood warnings that may be posted and note that in extreme and fortunately, very rare circumstances the river may be closed by the Gendarmes - you probably then wouldn't want to be on it, and Fluffy certainly would not - time to be safely entrenched in a local hotel, watching the floods though the window, with a re-assuring drink in one hand!

Planning your trip

When to go

This book is written mainly for those taking a summer holiday - which for most people means the school holiday period of July and August However, if you do have a choice of when to go in the year, then June is probably the best time, with wild flowers, hot sun, and good water levels.

The French summer vacation is two months long - almost the whole of July and August - however most families go away only from mid-July to mid August so this is high season and the prime time to avoid if you possibly can. If you are limited to UK summer holidays then a trip in late August is a good time as rivers, campsites, and tourist facilities are all quiet after the 14th August (note that the 15th August is like an unofficial New Year's Day with many facilities closed).

Climate

June, July and August are normally hot and sunny, with temperatures often in the 20's and sometimes the 30's. The higher up the rivers you are, then the cooler you will be (so the Allier, which is probably the highest river in this guide is probably the coldest - for both river and air temperature). Summer storms are rare, but can come at any time, bringing torrential rain and cold winds. They also bring the very rare (but real) risk of flooding.

Before you go

A little bit of time beforehand on reading and research can make your holiday a much better quality trip and save you time and money.

We suggest that you spend some time on the internet, and write off, or fax for information from tourist offices in the main centres that you are planning to visit. Also obtain up-to-date travel information from your motoring organisation or other source. If you are driving from Britain, then you should check with your car insurance company and extend the cover to other European countries if necessary.

Car breakdown insurance gives peace of mind but can be expensive. It's worth looking hard at the policies and doing a 'what if' scenario. If you do two or more trips a year then it's worth thinking about annual cover for the whole of Europe.

Medical cover

We recommend that you take out specialist medical and travel insurance for your trip to France. If you are involved in an accident and are injured it is likely that you will incur not only hospital charges, but also ambulance transfer fees and even helicopter call out fees in some cases. Serious accidents may also need subsequent air ambulance and repatriation to your home country.

Some general insurance policies will include canoeing cover but most exclude white water kayaking as they view this as high risk. So if you plan to paddle on class 2 or above then in our experience you are better talking to a specialist company (see the 'Suppliers Directory'). Policies bought direct from companies like these are normally much better value than those bought through second parties - in some parts of the travel industry the mark up on insurance can be as high as 100%.

If you travel regularly then an annual multi-trip policy is well worth considering, but again, do make sure that any high risk activities are specifically covered - it should also cover you if you break your leg one weekend hill walking!

France, like many European countries has a reciprocal health agreement with the U.K. A form DSS E111 (available from post offices) helps in administering medical expenses claimed back from the NHS in the U.K. and is a useful thing to have. This is particularly recommended if you choose not to take out travel insurance as it will help you claim back some of your medical expenses. But note that it is not an alternative to insurance, many hospitals and rescue services will still insist on you paying the bill or producing evidence of insurance.

What to take

Although the weather in the Massif Central is usually hot and sunny you should remember that there may be the occasional summer storm, so an umbrella and waterproofs are well worth packing.

The south of France can be very hot - up to 40 degrees - so it's worth planning for this. We take two ice boxes, one large one for the campsite (some families swear by a small portable fridge) and another one to go in the canoe. Most campsites will pop your freezer pack in their freezer for a small charge, so take several and mark them with your name.

Gorges du Tarn - picnic lunch in 'les Detroits'

One of the most useful items to take is a tarp or flysheet (with poles) so that you can rig this as a sun awning or rain fly. We take a table and folding stools that take up almost no room in the bottom of the boot, but there are some very comfortable folding armchairs available if you have the room. A hammock is another accessory that takes up little room but sets the right holiday tone!

French stores and supermarkets often have a wider range of camping accessories, like chairs and ice boxes, than your home camping store, and often substantially cheaper!

You will find that most foods that you can buy in your home country are available in France at roughly comparable or cheaper prices so it usually makes little financial sense to load your car down with food from home - you will eat much better if you buy fresh local produce, and this is surely one of the pleasures of a foreign holiday? You might want to consider though a stock of your favourite breakfast cereal and any other favourite speciality food: Brits will probably want to take fresh tea bags; Australians, vegemite; and Americans, peanut butter.

If you are a cycling family then one or more bikes are a great asset - they can be used for the car shuttle, fetching the morning bread, but also allow stroppy teenagers and frustrated adults to 'go off and do their own thing' and get a bit of space and time to themselves.

Sports sandals such as Tevas are really comfortable and healthy (banish smelly trainers to the car roof!). A French phrase book will pay for its cost many times over!

The joys of canoe camping

Next came the best bit - the start of true canoe camping - we moved the cars to the end campsite and would not see them again for 12 days.

At this point I made a decision. Our family had done enough work organising the trip, we weren't going to use more energy cooking every day. It was 4 days before Chris realised I wasn't being lazy when I scrounged water for morning tea and coffee, I'd deliberately left the stove in the car. Naturally, this strategy forced us to eat out in the evening but, at £7 or £8 for a 3 or 4 course meal who cares! (This is where creative accountancy comes in. Remember to ask your friends how much they paid for their package holiday, including the taxis and insurance they conveniently forget to mention, then calculate how much you've saved. Of course, on this basis you ought to be able to buy a new boat after every holiday but it never seems to work out that way. Oh well.....).

We would find a shady beach for lunch, or sometimes a large rock shelf carved out of the gorge by the river - the undercuts and holes created in the limestone by the river were like a geography lesson. Lunch nearly always consisted of the children of all ages swimming whilst baguettes were filled, then lazing away the rest of the 2 hour break.

Conditions were perfect. Good weather, 35 degrees, reasonable flow on the river and great company as we made our way towards Limeuil with rest days at Souillac and Beynac. There were a lot of shallow gravel rapids and one or two tricky bends just enough to add a little excitement to a wonderful holiday.

Lester Stuart

Canoe hire

As we mention elsewhere, canoe hire in France is cheap and easy, so it really makes sense to think about hiring rather than lugging a big open canoe half way across Europe. Several families we have talked to suggest that a nice compromise is to take 2 or 3 kayaks out from home so that some members of the family can use these for playing on white water, and then an extra open canoe can be hired for family day trips, or canoe camping. This also cuts down on all the ancillary gear like paddles, buoyancy aids, etc.

Security

Local people in country areas are honest and hard-working and in our experience you are less likely to have anything stolen than in your own home city. It is also worth saying that in thirty years of camping on French sites we have never had anything stolen - however you are on holiday so it does pay to take basic precautions - particularly when parking your car in cities or in busy tourist areas:

- Leave valuables in the safe keeping of your campsite guardian or hotel.
- Photocopy important documents (e.g. passport) and keep these separate.
- Take important phone numbers and money with you on the river in a waterproof pouch on your person.
- Take two cable locks so that you can lock boats (and cycles) both to your roof rack and if you leave any at your campsite.

(The worst incident we have heard of was some young kayakers who left their car in the South of France with everything in it and returned to find it had been stolen. The car had contained all their possessions, so they were left standing by the roadside in their swimming trunks, with no money, no clothes, no friends and no papers - the despairing cry 'mother' echoed up the lonely valley!)

Language

The French are proud of their language and culture so naturally they appreciate you attempting to use it, but these days all young people learn English at school and seem happy to practice it. We visited and spoke to quite a lot of tourist information centres and all had staff who spoke good English. Most canoe centres and kayak schools also had one member of staff who spoke some English - quite often someone who had paddled in New Zealand, Nepal, or North America - it's nice to see that white water paddling has become quite international!

Money

The introduction of the Euro has made travel in Europe so much easier. But, in truth you don't really need much cash - the French just love their Visa Cards 'la Carte Bleu' and it has become a nation that is almost more credit card friendly than North America. (forget about bringing travellers cheques). You will need cash for the occasional drink or campsite fee but this is easily obtained from a cash dispenser using either your credit or bank card, as long as you know your PIN number, or over the counter at larger banks (you will need your passport).

Note that UK credit cards will not work in most automatic 24 hour petrol stations, so don't run short of fuel when driving at night, or on Sundays.

Driving from the U.K.

Getting to the Massif Central from the UK involves about a 10-12 hour drive across France from the French channel ports. We strongly advise avoiding Paris by taking the more Eastern route through Reims and Dijon. Alternatively, consider a ferry to Dieppe or Le Havre and by-passing Paris on the west side

If you have 2 or 3 drivers then it's worth considering cruising the motorways through the night - we recommend that you leave room in the car so that you can stretch out when not driving. We normally switch drivers every two hours so that the driver is always fresh, and stop for coffee, toilet and petrol every four hours.

If you only have one driver, or a fractious family, then you might want to make an overnight break and the cheap hotel chains like Formule1 (20 euros for a room) are well worth considering (www.hotelformule1.com). Note though that French friends advise us that the car parks of these cheap hotel chains have a reputation for being insecure, partly because these chain hotels are often located in poor areas on the fringes of large cities - so a small family hotel in the country is usually better security and may be better value.

If you have a choice of vehicle, remember that in most of Europe, diesel fuel is a lot cheaper than petrol.

The different channel crossings all have their pros and cons. The ferry companies naturally want you to book long in advance, and usually offer discounts for so doing. In our experience substantially cheaper fares can be obtained through companies like Ferrysavers (www.ferrysavers.com) and it's worth pointing out that almost all tickets are in fact flexible, you can turn up for an earlier or later ferry, or chunnel, usually with no penalty or problem, so don't bust a gut just to get to your ferry on time. (I suppose one can be too blasé - I turned up once at Dover, presented my ticket and was told "but your ticket is for tomorrow Sir, from Ramsgate....." My girlfriend was not amused!)

Fluffy's top tip

Bikes (and especially the wheels) create a lot of air resistance when driving at speed, so we try to pack them inside the car for long journeys. If there are just two of us in a hatch back car like a Golf or a Fiesta, then we unclip the back seat backrest (easy when you know how) and take it out - this frees up a lot more room in the back of the car. We take the wheels, saddle, and pedals off the bikes and they then pack down beautifully in the bottom of the car for the journey to or from home.

When we get to France, it's just a ten minute job to re-assemble them and we find that for local journeys they then travel well on the roof, on top of the boats - nice and handy, so that at the top of the pass you can throw one off for a long downhill whoosh.

Driving in France

French roads are generally good and it's almost a pleasure to drive on their autoroutes (motorways). Short sections of autoroutes around the larger cities are usually free, but other motorways have toll charges that can be quite expensive, depending on your budget and the number in your vehicle. (for a private car it could cost you around 30 Euros in toll charges from Calais to the south of France, for a minibus, considerably more). Main trunk roads, called 'Route National' (RN) have improved considerably and are worth considering if you are on a budget and not in a mad rush. Minor roads are often bumpy and poorly marked so night driving on these can be as exciting as class 4 white water! Note that long stretches of the A20 and A75 autoroutes that cross the Massif Central from North to South, are free.

That the mainland Europeans drive on the right hand side of the road probably goes without saying. However, they do have a few other little quirks which are not so obvious. The main one is that traffic coming from the right has right of way. The exceptions to this are: roundabouts, motorways, and most main roads which are then marked as priority roads. This means that at all other times, typically in towns, when there are no signs and no road markings you must **give way to the right**.

There are also a few other legal requirements.

- You must carry your driving licence at all times when driving.
- You should carry a warning triangle and first aid kit in the car at all times.
- You must carry your vehicle registration document together with your insurance certificate. It is also advisable to carry a European Accident Statement which is normally supplied by your insurer.

Food and drink

France has its pizza, 'pomme frites' and MacDonald's. This is a country, however, which is still proud of its heritage of good food. Lorry drivers will sit down to a four course lunch at a 'Routiers' restaurant (worth looking out for) and French housewives still walk to the local market to buy their fresh produce. When in France, we recommend that you do as the French: have lots of barbecues and picnic style meals with salads and locally grown, fresh produce.

We suggest that you try to do most of your shopping in local markets and small shops rather than bland supermarkets as it's lots more fun, the food is much better, with superb flavoured quality produce, and remember, you will be both interacting with, and supporting local people. A boulangerie is a bread shop, and a patisserie is a fancy cake shop that often makes its own chocolates and ice cream - don't let anyone loose in here with the team kitty! A charcuterie is a pork butcher, but often more of a delicatessen, with freshly roasted chickens, pies, hams and sausages, freshly made salads, and mouth-watering quiches - great for picnic lunches or suppers - well, after a few bottles of wine, who feels like cooking?

Traditional, family-run restaurants usually serve delicious local cooking and in our experience offer excellent value - best is the 'table d'hote' fixed price meal. Sadly, after two weeks of all this temptation and good food, one vegetarian friend of ours succumbed and reverted to being a carnivore!

Fluffy and Charlotte shopping for ice cream

Where to stay

Camping

Most canoeists enjoy the outdoor life and camping is an obvious choice. French campsites are numerous, and good value. Almost all have hot showers and a wide variety of facilities and are graded from one to five stars. Typically in 2001 we were paying about 3 euros per head per night on a three star site. Some of the smaller, more attractive sites do get fully booked in the main summer holiday period but there are usually plenty of other local sites. If you plan to stay for a while then you may prefer to book ahead for peace of mind, and it is usually possible to select and reserve an individual pitch - the campsite will fax or mail you a site plan on request.

We have listed selected riverside sites in this book - we ourselves like simple, shady and quieter sites so we have tended to recommend these. Many of the sites we recommend are *'Camping au Naturel'* which indicates a less structured site, where your pitch is likely to be a tree in an old orchard rather than a hedged in patch of gravel. Another designation is *'Camping à la Ferme'* (farm sites) which are small simple sites. Tourist information offices have full listings of all sites and their facilities.

Several families we know with small children have booked holidays with companies such as Eurocamp, who provide not only all the camping tents and gear but also a full social programme to keep the kids amused. This saves you carting loads of camping gear with you half way across Europe - leaving room in the car for those important things like aquatic toys, and wine on the return! These are especially good value outside the school holiday period.

Huttes de France

Another crafty ploy to avoid all the hassles of packing and transporting camping gear is to rent a simple log cabin on a campsite. Some of the nicest sites have these - they are just a simple wooden chalet - a bit like a large summer house, with bunks, chairs, table, etc. so that you have all the enjoyment of camping without the hassle. These are a great idea if you are here early or late season when the weather may be wetter and cooler. More information from: www.chalet-decouvertes.com

Gites

Gites are self-catered French holiday cottages or houses. Local tourist offices can supply you with a list, or you can rent these through various commercial agencies in France and the UK. Note that Gites are often heavily discounted out of season, and well worth considering, because besides being warmer and drier, they may then actually be cheaper than camping

Gites d'Etape are something quite different - independent hostels (often with twin-bedded rooms and good food) that are ideal for small groups, particularly early or late season.

Hotels

French country hotels are incredibly good value typically being about half the price of what you would expect to pay in the U.K, so again well worth considering - Fluffy likes camping when the sun is shining, but he loves the ambiance of a traditional French country hotel - the restaurant, home-made ice cream.... etc.

Choice of Rivers

Planning your programme

It is difficult to recommend specific itineraries for the Massif Central rivers because everyone has very different desires and there is a wide variety of rivers. We suggest -

- Don't aim to do too much paddling - **give yourself time** - remember that there are many other enjoyable things to do in this beautiful region.
- If your aim is to paddle white water, then **build experience** and confidence on easier rivers before progressing to the more challenging ones.
- Allow for **flexibility** in your plans and adjust them if for example the weather turns bad or if local river conditions aren't good.
- Aim to build in **diversity** into your programme - so that you don't just paddle limestone gorges like the Tarn and the Ardèche.
- Arrange your itinerary to **limit driving time** - so that you drive from one river valley to the next around the periphery of the Massif Central. The drive across the mountainous heart makes a scenic and interesting journey, but is probably not one you want to repeat too often!

Canoe camping

This guidebook includes some of the best and most popular rivers in Europe for canoe camping - these are long, multi-day trips on beautiful rivers, with historic towns and villages, easy rapids to add interest, and lots of riverside campsites.

What makes it really easy is that a few canoe hire companies specialise in multi-day trips and will hire you all the gear for your trip - canoes, waterproof barrels, paddles, etc. They will also book your campsites for you if you wish, and then transport you back to the start and your car from where-ever you end up. All of this at such incredibly good value (an Old Town 17ft canoe cost us 50 Euros for 4 days) that many paddlers prefer to hire rather than have the hassle of transporting canoes from their home country.

If you have a choice then do try and plan your trip to avoid the summer peak season so that you miss the crowds. We ignored this advice and deliberately paddled all the rivers in this book in late July and early August. We didn't book our campsites ahead and although most looked full, all had a site or two free - even if technically full, we suspect that if you arrive by river, they will find you a spot.

Examples of the most popular canoe-camping rivers are:

Dordogne - 157 km of free-flowing, unspoilt river, almost no portages and typically done as a relaxed 10 day trip.

Allier - normally canoed as a one week trip 120km from Prades, but could be paddled from near its source, some 300km to its confluence with the Loire.

Célé - a small friendly river, ideal for young families, 48km and an easy a 3 day trip.

Lot - 150km through a beautiful valley but weirs on the bottom half.

Gorges de l'Ardèche - a famous, exciting, and spectacular 2 or 3 day trip.

Best rivers for young children

Please see our 'Fluffy' ratings, and as you know with kids, so much depends on the weather! However, on the basis that young children like easy, warm, smaller rivers with lots of interest and fun, then our recommendations would be to consider the following:

The Hérault (from Ganges) was a favourite with Thomas, William and Charlotte, and also the Tarn, with its beautiful clear, clean water and spectacular gorges. The Célé stands out as the perfect camping trip for young children. The Gorges de l'Ardèche would be a fantastic and exciting trip for older children whilst the Chassezac offers an easier and friendlier alternative. The Aveyron also deserves a mention, and then perhaps the classic stretch of the Lot from Entraygues, or some of the lower stretches of the Allier.

Best white water

Please see our star ratings for each run. One of our personal favourites was the Orb, probably closely followed by the Allier, which is noteworthy for its variety of whitewater runs. Then it would be hard choice between the Tarn or the Gorges de l'Ardèche. The **kayaker** looking for class 3 would enjoy the Vézère and stretches on the upper Allier - see the summary table.

Best for wildlife and wcenery

The most spectacular scenery is probably the limestone gorges of the Ardèche and the Tarn and if you go there in the quieter months you will be pleasantly surprised at the wildlife (beware the wild boar!). The Allier is probably top choice for the diversity of its fauna, scenery and wildlife whilst the Vézère deserves a mention for its understated, beautiful, quiet countryside.

Best for heritage and culture

All the rivers in this book have a wealth of historical villages, ancient châteaux, and fascinating places to explore, but the Dordogne stands out as the one river valley with a hugely rich historical heritage and many famous sights. Neighbouring river valleys to the west of the Massif Central - the Lot, Célé and Vézère could perhaps claim to have as equally rich a heritage.

Best weekend trip

Budget air flights, cheap car hire, and the ease of hiring canoes, means that a canoeing trip to the South of France is both easy to organise and relatively cheap. Examples might be to fly into Montpellier for a weekend on the **Orb**, to fly to St Étienne for a couple of days on the **Allier**, or to fly to Limoges for the **Vézère**. The Ardèche is probably not a good choice because it is always popular and crowded at weekends anytime June to September.

Rivers elsewhere

France is a large country and has a huge number of rivers suitable for canoeing, kayaking, and rafting - some 700 according to one guidebook. The French **Alps** is the most popular region for the white water enthusiast and the area also has a few easier rivers - see our guide book *'White Water Europe - South Alps'*). The rivers of the Pyrénées offer an alternative in early summer (see *'White Water Pyrénées'*). In the north of France are some pleasant flat water rivers noted for their scenery, ambience, and wildlife, for example: the Orne, Risle, Charente, and Eyre.

Books and Maps

General guidebooks

There are many guidebooks that cover different parts of the Massif Central but there appears to be no general guidebook in English devoted to the region as a whole.

The famous **Michelin Green Guides** are widely available and there are now English editions for most regions - you need to buy the relevant guide or guides for the rivers that you may be planning to paddle:

'Auvergne, Rhone Valley' - Allier and Ardèche

'Languedoc, Roussillon, Tarn Gorges' - Tarn, Hérault, Orb, Aveyron, upper Lot.

'Dordogne, Berry, Limousin' - Célé, lower Lot, Dordogne, Vézere.

The **Michelin Guide 'Camping Caravaning France'** is impressive and lists over 3000 selected sites with excellent detail. Waterside sites are especially highlighted.

There are numerous guidebooks about the Dordogne area (a new one seems to be published almost every year). We recommend the **Rough Guide to the Dordogne and Lot**, £9.99, published in August 2001. A popular older book to the same region is **The Three Rivers of France** by Freda White, Pavilion Books, ISBN 1 85145 7542.

Rough Guides also publish a more detailed guidebook to **Languedoc** which may be useful if you are planning a holiday in the area of the rivers Hérault and Orb.

There are more specialised local guidebooks available in French to particular local areas, these include hiking, mountain bike and climbing guides, and they are usually available for sale in local tourist information offices.

If you are considering a paddle on the lower stretches of the Lot and the Dordogne, or other navigations, then it is worth consulting Hugh McKnight's **Cruising the French Waterways**, 1999, £19.99.

Other canoeing guides

Canoe-Kayak Map of France. FFCK and IGN. 1993. Price 6 euros.

An excellent map that shows some 490 rivers, colour coded to show their difficulty; information is given in English, French and German; overprinted on a high quality and detailed road map of France at a scale of 1:1,000,000. Highly recommended and saves you buying a road map! Widely available in France from shops and motorway services stations.

Guide-Itineraires 700 Rivieres de France. Daniel Bonnigal. 1991. 22 Euros.

An impressively detailed guidebook to almost all the navigable rivers of France. A good reference source for those "what's that river like that we've just driven by?" enquiries. No maps & no illustrations give this a 5 mogadon rating for bedtime reading.

Rivers Occitanes, vol 1 & 2, by Puy Hardy cover almost all the rivers of the Massif Central and are good little guides that may be useful if you are paddling here in the spring or autumn when water levels are up and other rivers are flowing, however, these were last published and updated in 1985. Vol. 1 covers the Pyrenées, Orb and Herault; vol. 2 covers the Aveyron, Viaur, Lot, Célé, Dordogne and Vézère.

Local Guides - there are detailed canoeing guide books in French to most of the rivers in this book and we have noted these in the relevant river chapters, however many are more than ten years out of date.

Maps

I used to be a big fan of the Michelin big yellow road atlas of France at a scale of 1:200,000. At around £12 this is great value, but over the years I have got frustrated by the lack of topographical detail, and the sheer awkward size of it.

Perhaps a more practical buy is a big general road map of France - the AA one is very clear and easy to use and shows the difference between toll and non-toll motorways. I then recommend that you buy a more detailed map of the area that you intend to visit. Recommended best buys are the IGN TOP100 maps - these are published by the French Government mapping agency at a scale of 1:100,000. They show all roads, many tracks, rivers, streams, contour lines, tourist information, - all in lovely clear detail, and are ideal for car touring and cycling. They are widely available in France but only available from specialised travel outlets in the UK, e.g. Stanfords. www.ign.fr. www.stanfords.co.uk www.canotier.com

Websites

The internet is a great source of information. For general information on canoeing, kayaking, and the rivers in France try the website of the Federation Francais de Canoe Kayak, the FFCK - www.eauxvives.org.

Ray wondered why this river wasn't in the guide book - and why was that rock moving ...?

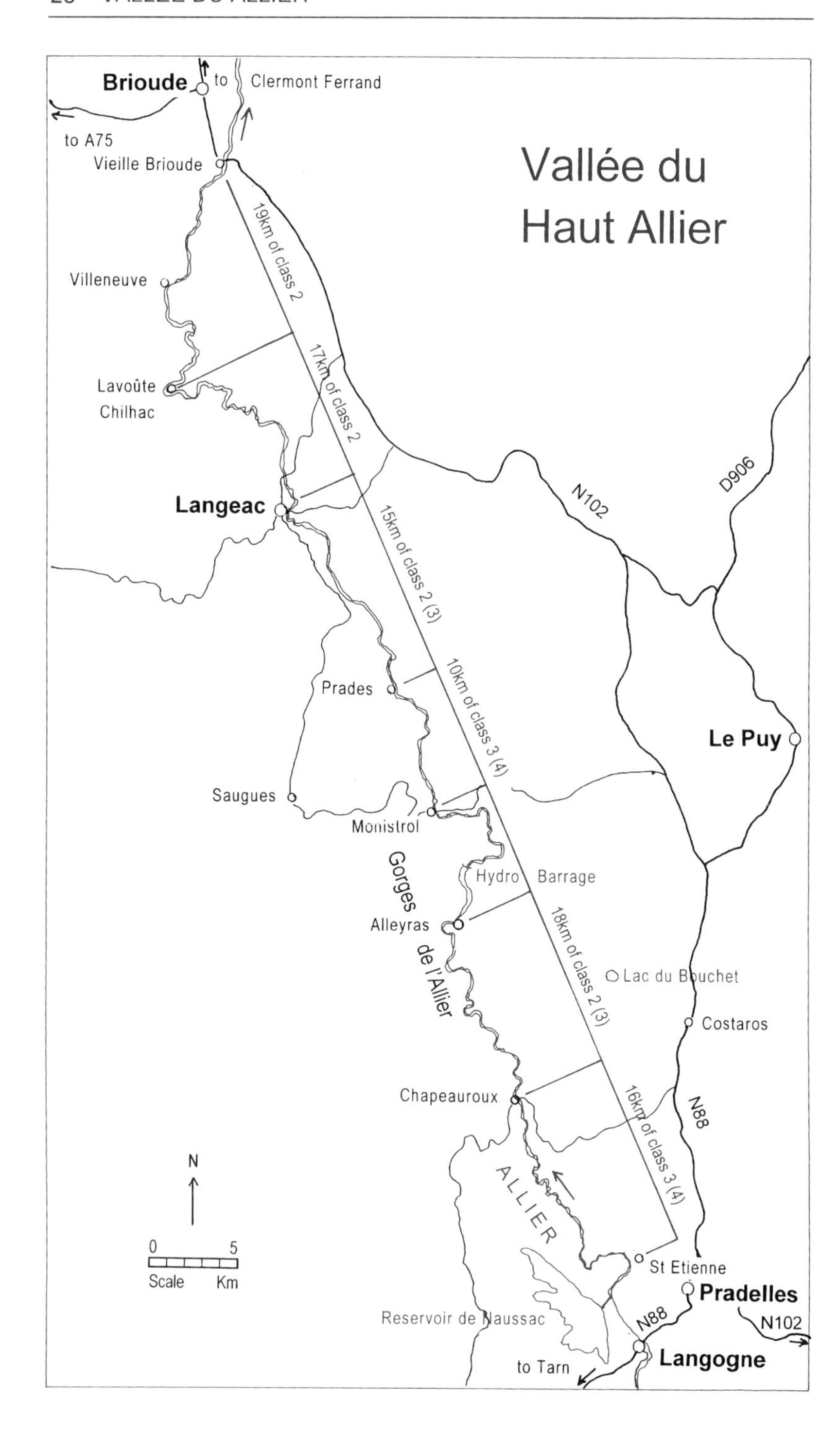
Vallée du Haut Allier
Brioude
to
Clermont Ferrand
to A75
Vieille Brioude
Villeneuve
Lavoûte
Chilhac
Langeac
Prades
Saugues
Monistrol
Gorges de l'Allier
Hydro Barrage
Alleyras
Lac du Bouchet
Costaros
Chapeauroux
ALLIER
St Etienne
Pradelles
Reservoir de Naussac
N88
N102
Langogne
to Tarn
Le Puy
N102
D906
N88
19km of class 2
17km of class 2
15km of class 2 (3)
10km of class 3 (4)
18km of class 2 (3)
16km of class 3 (4)
N
0
5
Scale
Km

Allier

Summary

Run	Class	Km	Stars	Scen.	Fluffy	Busy	Notes
St Etienne >	3 (5)	16	★★★	❁❁❁	-	<10	Technical, fun kayaking, very pretty.
Chapeauroux >	2 (3)	18	★★★	❁❁❁	☺	<50	'Jewel of a run' for canoes, fine gorge
Monistrol >	3-(3+)	10	★★	❁❁	-	<50	Good play boating and rafting run.
Prades >	2+	15	★★	❁❁	☺	<50	Pretty, scenic, friendly, canoe run. .
Langeac >	1-2	17	★★	❁❁	☺☺	<200	Old villages, granite cliffs, green river
Lavoûte Chilhac >	1-2	21	★★	❁❁	☺☺	<50	More of the same.
Brioude to Cournon	1(2)	67	★	❁	☺	<10	Pastoral & ideal canoe-camping.

The River

'The jewel of paddling in the Massif Central' is how many people have described this river. The Allier always had a reputation as scenic paddling river - but water levels were always too low to make it much of a paddle in the summer months. However this has all changed with the building of the huge Reservoir du Naussac up near its headwaters which now means a guaranteed flow all summer on the superb stretches of the magnificent volcanic Gorges de l'Allier. Excellent white water, guaranteed water levels, stupendous wild gorges and magnificent scenery make this a 'must do' if you are here in high summer. It's almost a shame to publicise such a fine river, particularly as it's relatively un-crowded.

River regulations

Part of the reason for this happy state is that there are regulations in place to protect the river and prevent its exploitation. We ask you to respect and adhere to these:

1. Paddling is restricted to **1000-1830** hours.
2. No more than 2 persons in a boat - Rafting and all craft with more than 2 persons are tightly controlled, only allowed on certain sections, and with prior permission.
3. Large groups are discouraged - there is a quota system to restrict the number of large groups on any section at any one time (parties of more than 4 persons must pre-book - tel: 71 77 28 30 - or call in at 'la Maison du Haut Allier', 42 Avenue Victor Hugo, in Langeac). In practice we suspect that a family group of say 6 persons is unlikely to cause offence - but if you have a club group of say 8 paddlers then you should split into two clearly separated teams
4. Access and egress is limited to authorised places - these are well signed with large wooden notice boards on the bank and small blue signs on the river.
5. The upper river is only open for navigation from 1st April to 14th October.

Water levels and temperature

The water levels can fluctuate because of the dam, and priority is given to releasing water in the high summer months, so you may get better water levels in say August than if you come here in May.

Water releases are usually around the 8 to 10 cumecs so this is not a big river. In character the middle river around Lavoute Chilhac is mellow and friendly and quite different to the upper river above Alleyras, which appears more like a wild Scottish Glen - transported to the hot sunshine of the Massif Central! In truth the upper Gorges besides being wild, feel appreciably colder. If a mid August cold front blows in with wind and rain then you might be better to pack up and head south for the Herault or the Orb.

Canoe Camping

The Allier is one of the classic canoe camping tours in Europe with good scenery, friendly, easy class 2 white water, and convenient campsites - ideal for a family open canoe trip. The favourite run is the 120 km from Prades to Cournon which can be done in a week. This can be extended (if you like flat water paddling) another week down to the confluence with the Loire at Nevers. The railway follows most of the valley, so it is possible to use this for the driver's shuttle; alternatively one of the commercial canoe operators can normally arrange this for you, along with canoe hire if needed.

Off the river

This region of Auvergne is one of rolling landscapes, volcanoes, green forests, ancient villages - half deserted, blue skies and distant horizons. Traditionally one of the poorer regions of France and until recently, one that saw few tourists. There has been a big effort in recent years to rectify this and to promote the natural beauty and attractions of the area, with promotion for new tourist enterprises. So there's lots of new lively eco-tourism companies eager to take you ballooning, climbing, gliding, rafting, mountain biking, horse riding, etc - all at very reasonable prices when compared to more touristy areas like the Dordogne.

A nice example of these new tourism initiatives is the Velo-Rail at Pradelles. This is a little cycle trolley that you propel along an old railway line over-looking the Gorges de l'Allier, clattering along the rails, over viaducts, and shooting in and out of tunnels. You need to phone to book this a day or two ahead - 04 71 00 87 46. This is also an excellent area for mountain and road cycling with a wide choice of routes over the rolling landscapes of Auvergne - most of the canoe shuttles also make very pleasant bike rides.

This region is famous for its volcanic features and on the drive to the upper valley, we recommend that you take time to visit the Lac du Bouchet, which is the best example of a circular volcano crater lake in Europe - just 2km off the road to Alleyras and complete with bar and pedaloes.

The tourist season tends to be short here - mainly July and August so some restaurants and campsites may be closed early season. The tourist offices below have a host of useful leaflets on these and other ideas.

Food and drink

This area of the Haut Allier is a bastion of good French cooking at old fashioned prices - it hasn't been spoilt by too much tourism and we had some great meals out! We mention some recommendations in the text, but if we had to select just one, it has to be *l'Auberge de Vallee'*, a 'Logis de France' hotel and restaurant in St Haon, near Chapeauroux. Tel:71 08 20 73.

Camping

There's a good choice of campsites up and down the valley, most offering excellent facilities at pleasantly cheap prices. The river is long and some driving shuttles can be tortuous so if you want to do day trips out of your campsite, then we recommend that you consider two bases, for example Chilhac and Alleyras, to cut down on the driving. Most of the sites were spacious and un-crowded when we visited, so it's not really necessary to book months in advance, if at all.

Chapeauroux - 'Camping les Eaux Vives', tel: 66 46 33 37.
Alleyras - Camping Municipal, tel: 04 71 57 58 59.
Monistrol - Municipal le Vivier, tel: 04 71 57 24 14.
Prades - J'aux'vie, Tel: 04 71 74 00 41.
Langeac - Camping le Pradeau, tel: 04 71 77 05 01.
Chilhac - Aire Naturelle de Camping, tel: 04 71 77 46 65.
Lavoûte Chilhac - La Ribeyre, tel: 04 71 77 48 03
Villeneuve - la Vialette, tel: 04 71 74 72 11
Brioude- Camping - Camping la Bageasse, tel: 04 71 50 07 70
Brassac les Mines - tel: 04 73 54 30 88
Nonette - Camping Les Loges 04 73 71 65 82
Issoire - Camping Municipal, tel: 04 73 89 03 59
Cournon - le Pre des Laveuses, tel:04 73 84 81 30.

Haut Allier - a rapid below Monistrol

Maps and Guides

IGN Top 100 sheet 48 covers the whole of the Haut Allier at a scale of 1:100,000 so is our recommended best buy. IGN 1:25,000 sheet 2736O covers the river from Chapeauroux to beyond Monistrol, and sheet 2635E from Prades to Chilhac, so these are worth considering for local walks and bike rides if you are staying in the area.

There is a recently re-published Topo-guide *'Eaux vives du Haut Allier'*, which is well worth buying if you are spending time in the valley. This doesn't cover the river below Brassac les Mines, however a somewhat similar booklet *'Rivière d'Auvergne'* covers the lower Allier and rivers like the Loire. These should be available from larger tourist offices and le Canotier.

Tourist Offices -

Le Puy en Velay, tel: 04 71 02 02 15, www.ot-lepuyenvelay.fr
Pradelles, tel: 04 71 00 82 65 www.pradelles.com
Langeac, tel: 04 71 77 05 41 ` email: ot.langeac@haut-allier.com
Lavoûte-Chilhac, tel: 0471 77 46 57
Brioude, tel: 04 71 74 97 49
Issoire, tel: 04 73 89 15 90

Canoe Hire and rafting

Alleyras - Planete Congagny, tel: 04 71 74 46 71
Monistrol - A.N. Rafting, tel: 04 71 57 23 90 www.an-rafting.fr
St Privat - Riviere Trek, tel: 04 71 57 22 54
Langeac - Tonic Aventures tel: 04 71 77 25 64 www.tonic.aventure.fr
Chilhac - Euro Rivière, tel: 04 71 77 43 66, ww.euroriviere.com
Lavoûte-Chilhac - Canoe Rad'eau, tel: 04 71 77 47 88
- Safaraid, tel: 04 71 77 44 80
Villeneuve - Sportival, tel: 04 71 74 70 42
Brioude - Cap'Vacances, tel: 0471 50 00 70

Other rivers

There are no other rivers in the area that are likely to have any white water in the summer months. The **Loire** might seem an obvious possibility but much of the water in its upper reaches is captured by a reservoir at la Palisse and diverted south through an aqueduct to augment the flow of the Ardèche. Paddlers living in the Loire valley are understandably annoyed about this! Nearest other summer rivers are the Ardèche, Tarn, and Lot.

Ringed Plover

rges de l’Ardèche ‘les Trois Eaux’ rapid.

Image Actions

Surfing on the Allier, below Chapeauroux. Kate Ban

Jonchères Bridge on the upper Allier.

ɔrges de l'Ardèche - wild boar crossing the river. mage Actions

ɔrges de l'Ardèche - Pont d'Arc.

Gorges de l'Ardèche -'la Pastière' rapid and 'la Cathedrale' back in the permissive 70's.

Allier below Prades.

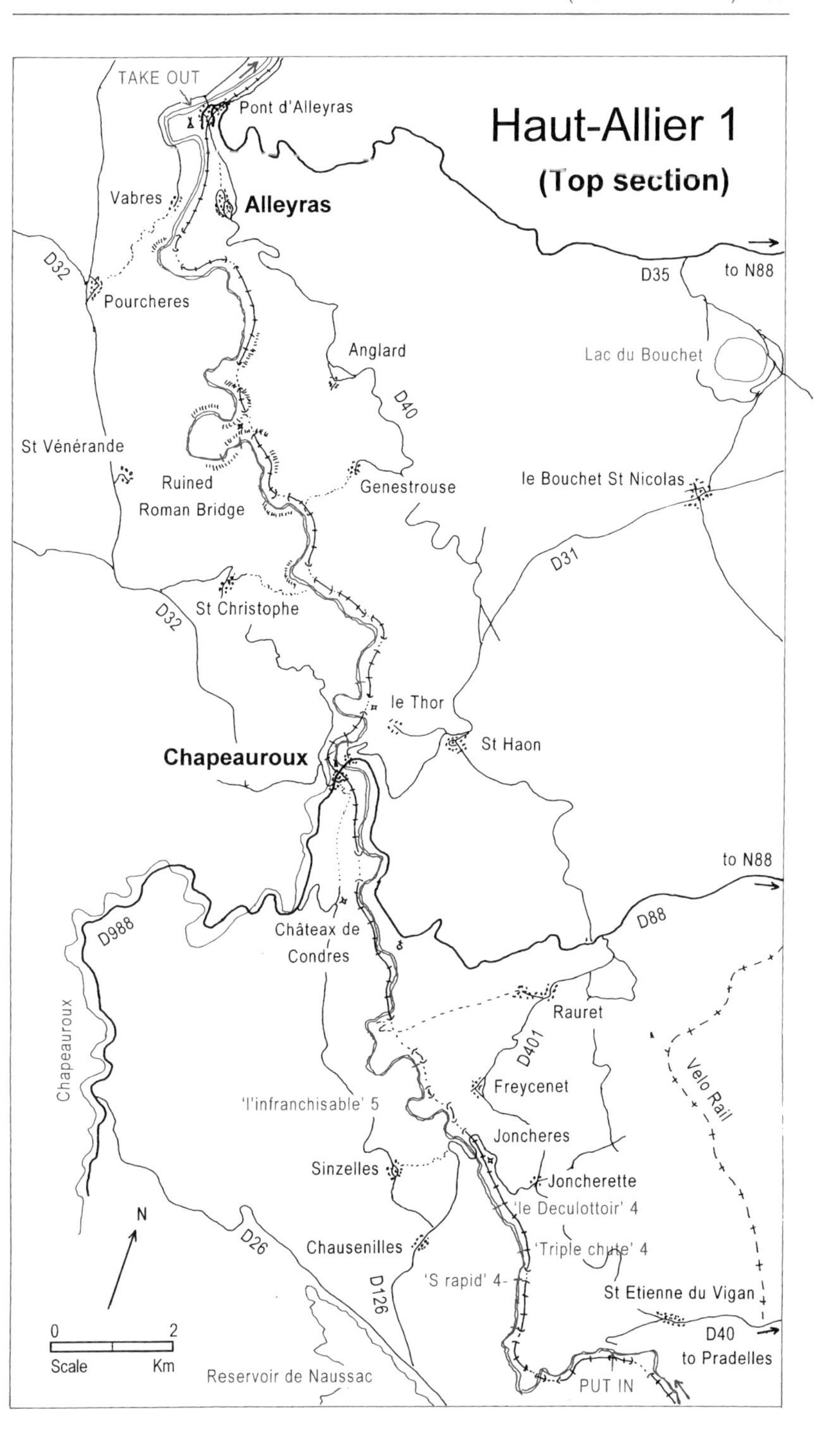

Haut-Allier 1
(Top section)
TAKE OUT
Pont d'Alleyras
Vabres
Alleyras
D32
Pourcheres
D35
to N88
Anglard
Lac du Bouchet
D40
St Vénérande
Ruined
Roman Bridge
Genestrouse
le Bouchet St Nicolas
D31
St Christophe
D32
le Thor
St Haon
Chapeauroux
to N88
D88
D988
Châteax de
Condres
Rauret
D401
Chapeauroux
Velo Rail
Freycenet
'l'infranchisable' 5
Joncheres
Sinzelles
Joncherette
'le Deculottoir' 4
N
Chausenilles
D26
'Triple chute' 4
'S rapid' 4-
D126
St Etienne du Vigan
D40
to Pradelles
0
2
Scale
Km
Reservoir de Naussac
PUT IN

St Etienne to Chapeauroux	**16 km of class3 (5)**	★★★	❀❀❀	-
Water quality - excellent	Temperature - cool		Busy?	<10

St Etienne to Jonchères 6km, class 3 (4), then to Chapeauroux 10km class 3 (5).

Summary

This is perhaps the prettiest stretch of the Allier, crystal clear water flows over a sandy bottom, with pink granite boulders, sage and pine hillsides, and little yellow beaches nestling between low cliffs. The paddling is mainly class 2 and 3 and a lot of fun with heaps of little eddies and play waves (there are few flat stretches and it never drops below class 2). The section down to Jonchères has three rapids that probably deserve a class 4 rating and then it's a steady class 3 run down to Chapeauroux with just the one grade 5 rapid that is harder. We saw wild boar and otter prints, and lots of fish and birds - including what we think were ospreys and buzzards. The railway follows the valley, diving in and out of tunnels, but is out of sight of the river for most of the time.

This is a friendly, fun paddle for kayakers, but probably a bit too technical and challenging for most canoeists - some of the grade 3 rapids are long and would probably swamp most open canoes (unless you had a spraydeck). Fluffy sensibly decided not to do this top stretch, as it sounded like he would get wet, and instead relaxed on the campsite - probably a wise move in that none of the smaller villages even had an ice cream, only Chapeauroux and St Haon have shops.

Shuttle

A narrow tarmac road leads down to the put-in below the village of **St Etienne** du Vigan. There is room to park a few cars at the end of the road and from here a rough path leads steeply down to the river. The shuttle is very scenic, with lovely vistas over the rolling countryside of Auvergne. The full shuttle is best done on the East bank on D401, but if you are doing a cycle shuttle just between Jonchères and Chapeauroux, then the country lanes on the west bank make a very pleasant and picturesque bike ride.

Description

The river starts off as class 2+, bubbling little rapids, and in the middle of the river are little islands of wild flowers and pink granite boulders topped with great tuffs of long grass hanging down like untidy hair cuts. Sue said that this reminded her of the North Island of New Zealand and rivers like the Rangitaki. However, looking up from the river gives the lie to this, with pine trees, heather, and gorse - making this granite valley more reminiscent of some Scottish river like the Findhorn.

A fine little rocky gorge follows the railway viaduct with a little play wave and class 3 shoot at the end. Then there is a railway embankment wall on the right, and after a km and roughly in line with the third railway tunnel is *'S bend'* rapid, a technical, , class 4- boulder maze. 300m of flat water is an obvious warning for *'Triple chute'* - 3 distinct drops with thought provoking stoppers making it a fair class 4. Land right to inspect.

After another 300m of flat water you can see the ruins of Jonchères castle up on the skyline ahead and this warns you of *'Le deculottoir'* (roughly translates as 'the hammering'!) - an easy class 4 boulder ramp dropping 2m and normally run centre.

It is then a kilometre of mainly class 3 paddling to **Jonchères** bridge, where there is a access on the right below the bridge. There's a beautiful golden yellow beach here, so on hot days in the summer this is a favourite picnic and bathing spot that rivals Baywatch. Jonchères is not a village, but just an ancient bridge over the river, a disused railway halt, beach and put-in, with a small car park, toilet and changing hut. The river continues from here as a bubbling class 2 and then the first class 3 rapid is after 2km on a tight right hand bend, as the valley becomes more of a gorge.

After this, keep your eyes open right for the railway line popping out of a tunnel, onto a bridge over a side stream, and then back into a tunnel again. **'L'infranchisable'** rapid is about 250m below here, next to a prominent railway embankment wall and cliff face on the right. There's one class 3 rapid in this 250m approach, then a 30m flat stretch and a small yellow beach on the left. This is the safest place to land and inspect, because after this a class 3 rapid leads you down into the maws of *'the unrunnable one'* (These days, most expert paddlers would consider it very runnable - it's probably a class 5 or a 4+, depending on water levels). The rapid finishes with a class 3+ drop and then there is a big house rock in the middle of the river. For the nervous, this all adds up to maybe a 100m portage, over small boulders, or maybe 30m for the more confident.

Allier - looking upstream at Chapeauroux: viaduct, campsite and village.

From here on the river keeps going at a fair pace, with lots of white water interest, and all in a wild gorge with few signs of civilisation. The rapids are mainly class 2 with a few class 3 to keep you on your toes, but nothing harder than this. The railway viaduct marks the half way point. Two km of more fine white water and the little chapel of St Médard is visible on the knoll on the right. Another 2 km and the road is close, the valley widens a bit, the river is now less constrained and has several long shallow, rocky rapids that are a disappointment and an anticlimax after what has gone before.

Take out on the left bank at **Chapeauroux,** 100m downstream of the bridge - just at the entrance to *'Camping les Eaux Vives'* - a well-managed site, with good modern facilities, but small and often crowded. There's a locals bar across the road, and 3km up the road in St Haon is a restaurant and hotel that we can heartily recommend - *'l'Auberge de Vallee'*.

Chapeauroux to Alleyras	**18 km of class 2 (3)**	★★★	❀❀❀	☺
Water quality - good	Temperature - cool		Busy? <50	

Summary

One of our favourite runs in an open canoe - 'the Jewel in the Crown' for paddling in the Massif Central! Nearly 40 rapids in all, continuous class 2 white water, with a few easy class 3 rapids, all in a beautiful wild gorge, assured water levels, crystal clear water, and the hot sunshine of southern France - what more could you want? (Ice cream and cold beer at the take out?....) Like the gorges upstream, this is very Scottish in character with clear water flowing between pink granite boulders, pine covered hillsides, and the occasional yellow beach nestling between low cliffs. There are lots of wild flowers, fish and bird life. The railway follows the valley, but in no way intrudes on the experience. Despite the quality of this run, you will meet relatively few paddlers - typically one commercial group of 'hot dogs' and say 6 other paddlers.

The run is ideal for competent open canoeists, or competent but nervous kayakers wanting to build experience. The French companies take groups down with a Moniteur and use open canoes or inflatable 'hot dogs'

Shuttle

If you are driving from afar, then the drive into Alleyras or Chapeauroux is magnificent, with rolling vistas of the Auvergne countryside and then a steep descent by narrow, twisting roads into the hidden gorges of the Allier. (Take time to call in at the Lac du Bouchet, 2km off the road, - a perfectly round lake in the middle of an extinct volcano.) The connecting road from Alleyras to Chapeauroux, the D40, is twisting, scenic and climbs up some 300m above the river. Probably takes 40 minutes driving or a couple of hours cycling?

Your driver may well be able to get a lift back with one of the commercial companies - however, the classic and fun way to do this shuttle is on the railway! There is usually a convenient train around 1800, which fits in fine if you are camping at Alleyras (check before though, as some trains don't run on public holidays).

The camping site at le Pont d'Alleyras can be highly recommended as an ideal family base, spacious, shady, good facilities and close to the river where there is a safe beach and flat water for swimming. It's just 5 minutes walk into the small village where there's a good little supermarket, and a choice of two bars and restaurants. There are also some little wooden cabins for rent.

Description

At **Chapeauroux**, put on at the embarkation point 100m downstream on the left bank (Take the first turn sharp right over the bridge). The Chapeauroux river joins from the left - take two minutes to look back at the impressive sweep of the famous **Chapeauroux viaduct.** As you paddle round the bend ahead you come to the first class 3 rapid and this sets the standard for the run - always reassuring to know, and if you're really not happy at this stage, now is the time to take out on the right and walk back the short way to the village, rather than press on into the trackless, wild gorges ahead!

High up above the cliffs ahead are the ruins of the fortified tower of Le Thor, guarding the river crossing. The railway line swoops over the river, and then disappears into a tunnel beneath the cliffs, and then for the next 16 km it pops in and out of tunnels some 13 times. You paddle round the bend, the cliffs grow higher, the valley sides narrow in on the river, and there's no doubt that you are now entering the 'Gorges de l'Allier'. You will see the railway again on the right and then shortly after, there's a class 3 rapid - when we were here this was best taken down the centre shoot, as the right goes into rocks and trees.

The river keeps up its pace with some long,·bouncy class 2+ wave train rapids - we did a lot of bailing on this run and Fluffy retired to a seat in the middle of the canoe rather than his favourite spot at the front! A rare bit of pasture field on the left marks where a path goes up to the little village of St Christophe - a possible emergency egress; and after a km there is another possibility where a path from Genestouse comes down to the big railway embankment on the right.

Another km and if you can lift your eyes from the rapids, you will see the ruins of an old castle on the hill top ahead. This marks another nice long bouncy class 3 rapid that takes you round the left hand corner ahead and brings you down to the **Ruined Roman Bridge** and a pool and beach in which to salvage any swamped boats. This marks the **half way point** in terms of distance, is a beautiful spot, and so a favourite lunch spot. All the class 3 rapids are now behind so it's a time to relax and chill out.

Below here is perhaps the most dramatic and scenic part of the gorges with the rivers twisting and turning under high cliffs. Good class 2, 2+ rapids continue with some playful shoots and wave trains. After some 5km the civilisation impinges just a little - the village of Alleyras can be seen on the hill ahead, then the river does a big curve and the little village of Vabres is close on the left. Take out 2km further, beyond the 'Village Vacances' at the public beach next to the campsite.

Don't be tempted to continue, as the next section of river has a huge hydro dam on it, so all access is forbidden until Monistrol.

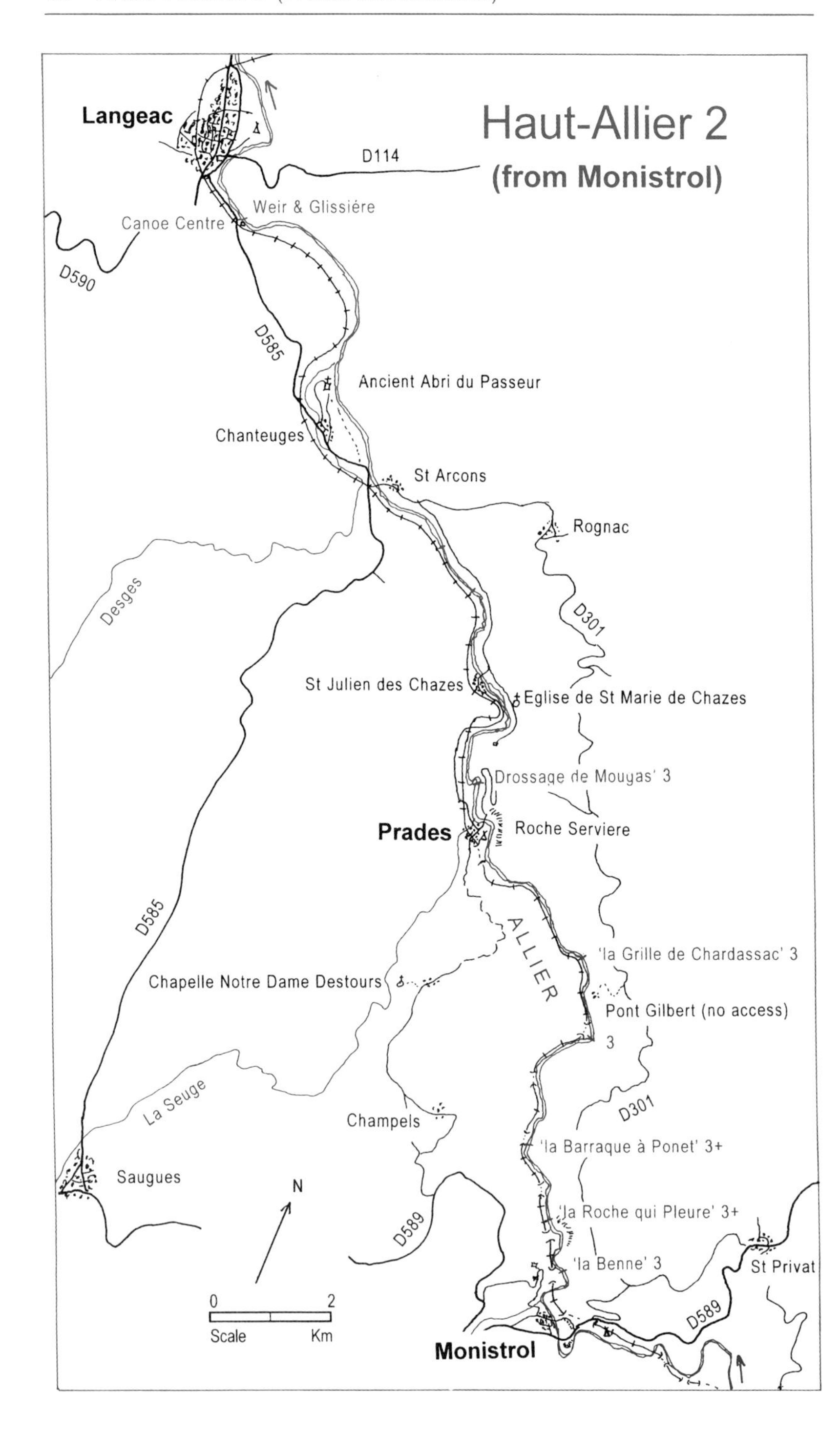
Haut-Allier 2
(from Monistrol)
Langeac
D114
Weir & Glissiére
Canoe Centre
D590
D585
Ancient Abri du Passeur
Chanteuges
St Arcons
Rognac
Desges
D301
St Julien des Chazes
Eglise de St Marie de Chazes
'Drossage de Mouyas' 3
Prades
Roche Serviere
D585
ALLIER
'la Grille de Chardassac' 3
Chapelle Notre Dame Destours
Pont Gilbert (no access)
3
La Seuge
D301
Champels
'la Barraque à Ponet' 3+
Saugues
N
'la Roche qui Pleure' 3+
D589
St Privat
'la Benne' 3
0
2
Scale
Km
D589
Monistrol

Monistrol to Prades **10 km of class 3- (3+)** ★★ ❁❁ -

Water quality - good Temperature - cool Busy? <50

Summary

A fine white water run with lots of interesting rapids in the first half of the run, in another deep wild gorge (but not as dramatic as the ones upstream). This run feels like a bigger river, and perhaps it is, because it's certainly used for commercial rafting. In low water, normal summer levels the run is mainly an easy class 3 with a few rapids that are class 3+, its mainly pool drop, so there's time to get your breath back. The rapids are often formed by big boulders so it's a fun river for route finding, but all very straight forward, lines are fairly obvious and there's nothing especially difficult or dangerous (it compares well with the run on the Vézere Gorge). The French guides rate this run as a class 3 (4) but this is probably to allow for higher water levels in early summer or perhaps to make the rafting sound more exciting than it perhaps is!

This is a fine river for kayak play, with plenty of little surfing waves and endo spots. We were tempted to try it in an open canoe, but the problem is 2 or 3 long wave train rapids (200m or so long) where an open canoe would probably swamp on the first drop. It's a popular stretch for kayaking, 'les hot dogs' and rafting so expect to see other paddlers and a couple of commercial trips on this stretch. The last 4 km are class 2, with long flat stretches, and a definite wind down.

Shuttle

The shuttle drive is along the D301 on the right hand valley side with fine views over the gorges. Allow half an hour driving - the road climbs about 200m above the river so it's not too bad as a cycle shuttle - 1½ hours maybe? This is a reasonably popular stretch for commercial companies so you may be able to get a lift. If you fancy an even more scenic and adventurous drive, then we recommend the very narrow road along the ridge on the valley left, via the little commune of la Vialle Destours (the picturesque chapel of Notre Dame d'Estours is just off this road).

Description

Monistrol is an old village located at one of the ancient trading routes across the Allier Gorges. There's two restaurants, a few shops, a station and a campsite (upstream on the right bank).

Put in at Monistrol on the left bank downstream of the old steel bridge. (Note paddling is illegal upstream of the campsite in Monistrol because of the hydro-electric power station and dam). The Ance stream joins from the left after 200m and forms the first rapid - this is normally typical for the run - so if you're really not happy now is the time to pull out before you enter the 'gorges of no return'! Most paddlers will be salivating with delight and anticipation and the next little succulent treat is just round the bend and downstream of the railway bridge. The locals call this *'La Benne'* which roughly translates as 'dump truck' - really a big dump of rocks in the river and usually with a shoot on the right. This is followed by *'la Table'* - a large table like rock in the middle of the river with the usual route to the left.

Another couple of bends, and just under a km of easier rapids brings you down to *'la Roche qui pleure'* (the 'Rock that cries), which is marked by a conical rock on the left - a class 3+ fun shoot with a big wave (the crying rock is on the river right and sometimes has the appearance of a large nose with streams of tears running down each side). Another km of bouncy little rapids brings you to a long sweeping railway enbankment wall on the left, and at the end of this is *'la Barraque à Ponet'*, a big long rapid, nearly 400m long with 3 distinct evenly spaced drops, and a big round boulder to avoid at the bottom (the kind that a swamped open canoe would just fold round ever so neatly....).

By now, you have the flavour of this river, - a light succulent dish, with tasty morsels, but no indigestible or chewy lumps, - it's just one juicy bite after another for 3km - all at the bottom of this wild green gorge, with buzzards circling overhead, and the only sign of civilisation being occasional glimpses of the railway line.

The little commune of **Pont Gilbert** on the right is a warning that the best is nearly over. There's no access or egress here unless in case of emergency. All is not over, for a km further on is another bouncy class 3 rapid 'la Grille de Chardassac' that marks the portal to the end of the gorge. After this the valley widens out, the river flatten out with just the occasional class 2 rapid, and it's just 2km to the village of Prades.

Everything seems to be over, but not the scenery, because as you come around the bend you have this superb view ahead of these amazing cliffs formed of basaltic columns, perched some 100m high above the river. Float along and then take out upstream of the public beach (and well upstream of the bridge) - look out for the many swimmers, and of course a busy beach like this has to have a friendly riverside bar that sells ice creams!

Prades is a busy little holiday village with a good boulangerie, shop and two bars and restaurants. Mansur Darlington recommends the small friendly campsite just upstream from here: 'le Jeaux 'vie' is in a stunning location, but this is definitely a 'Camping Naturelle' site with a rough track for access, and primitive facilities, however,it does have a couple of llamas! Tel: 04 71 74 00 41.

Allier - basalt cliffs and the bridge at Prades.

Prades to Langeac	**15 km of class 2+**	★★	❁❁	☺
Water quality - reasonable	Temperature - warm		Busy? <50	

Prades to St Arcons 8km, Langeac 7km.

This is a pretty, scenic and popular stretch of the river with wooded banks, green hillsides, and grey basalt cliffs. Although the road and railway are close for most of the way, there are only glimpses, and it feels wilder than it actually is. The paddling is mainly class 1 and 2, with a few rapids that are slightly harder - the first one of these can be easily portaged. The river is wide and there are pools and flat stretches between the rapids in which to relax and recover. The second half of the run, after St Arcons is less interesting, so many people take out here.

Prades is the popular start point for multi-day canoe camping trips so this is a popular stretch and you will see a lot of boats, also on hot days, a lot of bathers and people having picnics by the riverside.

Shuttle
The road follows the valley bottom so shuttles are quick, convenient and also pleasant by cycle.

Description
Put in at the public beach in **Prades**, upstream of the bridge, river left. One kilometre brings you to the 'Drossage de Prades' where the river makes a tight turn and the current sweeps under the cliffs on the right. If this is your first time on the river and you are starting here, you may want to land left and make an easy portage, rather than risk a capsize on this technical little rapid (which may be a class 3 in higher water).

Another kilometre brings you to le Pradel farm, where there is a beach and landing place on the right. The river then settles into a more lively pace with class 2 rapids every km - nothing technical, but some long ones so in higher water, the waves could swamp an open canoe. Around the next bend the Romanesque Chapel of Ste Marie stands in a beautiful riverside setting and the rapids take you down to the bridge at St Julien-des-Chazes

About a km before St Arcons, but out of sight of the village, is a class 2+ rapid on a right hand bend, where the current sweeps into some rocks on the left. **St Arcons** then comes into sight on the hillside right, with pretty roofs and granite walled houses. There is no landing here, but a further km brings you to a public beach, river left, below the village of **Chanteuges**, whose church now dominates the valley. You can take out at this beach. Road access is upstream via a metalled track which joins the road near St Arcon Bridge. A part of this flat area has been set aside for camping sauvage. Follow the signs for 'Aire Naturelle de Camping'. More basic than basic, the area does nevertheless boast a two hole toilet hut and a tap!

The river stays pretty with basalt cliffs dropping directly into the water. There follow two long, bouncy rapids that might even be class 2. These bring you to the remains of the Abri du Passeur (Ferryman's Shelter), shortly followed by the Desges stream joining left (The new building on the stream is a salmon breeding and research station). Now the river becomes wider, the current eases, and there is just the occasional class 1 rapid running over shingle bars.

The riverside is lined with meadows, tall trees, woodland, and the occasional sandy beach, but still no sign of houses or civilisation, until after 4km, you come round the bend and there are the buildings of the Langeac Canoe Kayak Base on the left. You can take out here, or continue another km down to the town and the campsite below the bridge. If you decide to continue you need to either portage the weir at the base, or shoot it by the photogenic **glissière** on the right hand side. Check this out carefully first!

Langeac is a large town with all the facilities that you would expect and makes a good base for exploring the valley. The 3 star municipal campsite extends for nearly a km down the riverside and has 200 emplacements, so is rarely crowded. It's spacious, shady, and has facilities like swimming pool, bar, etc. This is deservedly a popular site with paddling families.

Allier below Prades - the Chapel of Sainte Marie des Chazes.

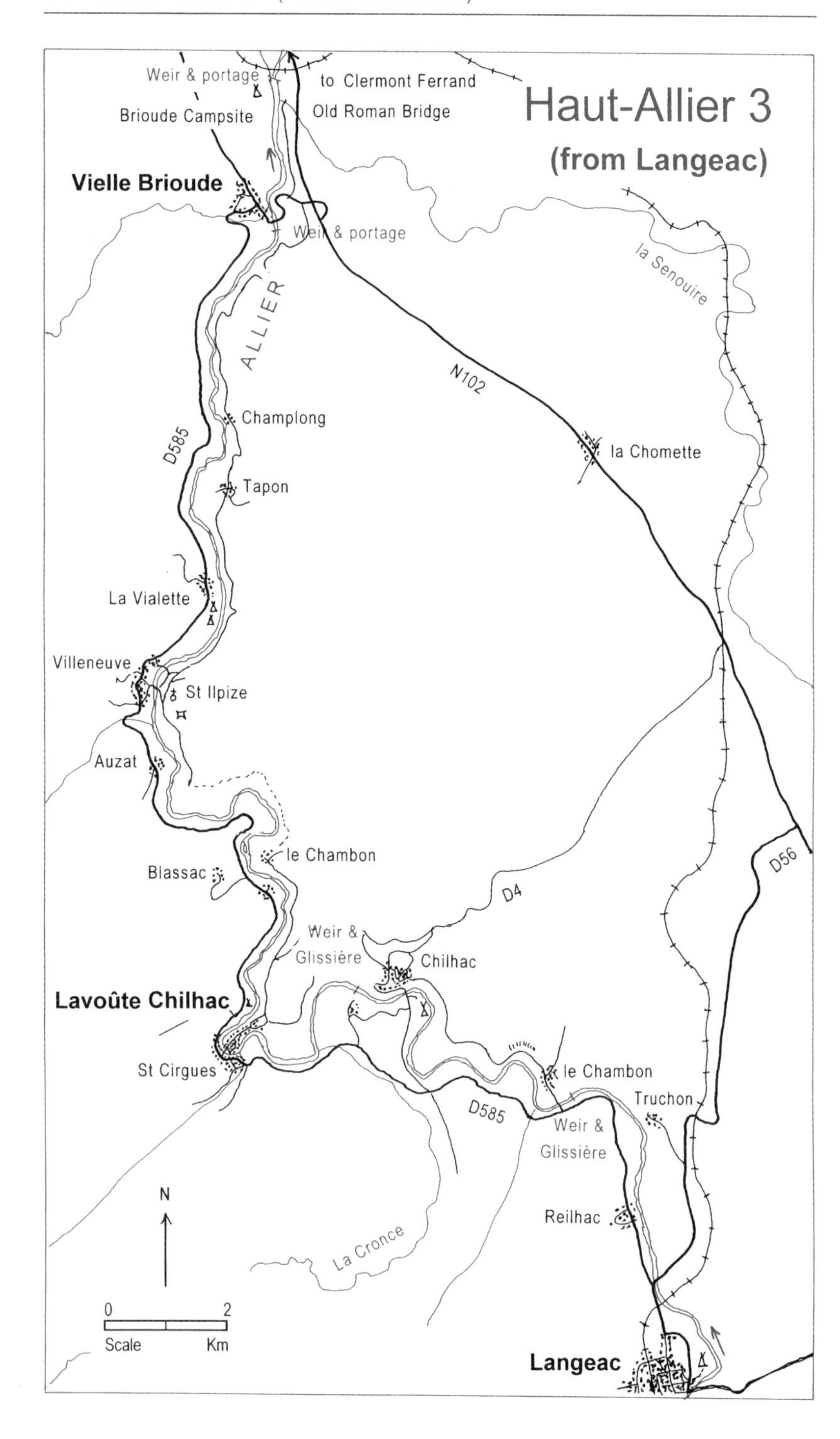
Haut-Allier 3
(from Langeac)
Weir & portage
to Clermont Ferrand
Old Roman Bridge
Brioude Campsite
Vielle Brioude
Weir & portage
la Senouire
ALLIER
N102
Champlong
D585
Tapon
la Chomette
La Vialette
Villeneuve
St Ilpize
Auzat
le Chambon
Blassac
D4
D56
Weir &
Glissière
Chilhac
Lavoûte Chilhac
St Cirgues
le Chambon
Truchon
D585
Weir &
Glissière
N
Reilhac
La Cronce
0
2
Scale
Km
Langeac

Langeac to Lavoûte Chilhac **17 km of class 1-2** ★★ ❁❁ ☺☺

Water quality - ok Temperature - warm Busy? <200

Langeac to le Chambon 6km, Chilhac 6 km, Lavoûte Chilhac 5 km.

Summary

A pleasant stretch with good scenery in the second half. The paddling is mainly class 1, with just a couple of class 2 rapids to give interest, also an entertaining and technical glissière at le Chambon. This is popular for people hiring canoes so you will meet quite a lot of boats - probably not a 100, but getting near that figure - also on a hot sunny day you will encounter a lot of bathers. This is quite different to the upper gorges and definitely not a wilderness paddle.

Shuttle

This is an easy shuttle and for once the road distance is less than the river.

Description

Put in at the campsite downstream of the bridge in Langeac. Alternatively if you want to make a shorter run, then we suggest starting at Le Cambon. A kilometre after the campsite is the railway bridge, shortly followed by a road bridge, and then some 500m after here are 2 bouncy class 2 rapids that bring you down level with Reilhac village on the left. After another km the river widens out near Truchon, with 3km of mainly flat 'dog water' leading down to the weir at le Chambon. There is a glissière on the left, with a shallow rapid below. This requires quite a technical move to shoot it safely so we recommend that you stop on the left bank above and inspect. If you have any doubts, then the portage is an easy and safe option.

Le Chambon has a public beach and landing on the right bank 300m downstream from the bridge (reached by a small lane). As you go round the bend from this beach you will see ahead a line of basalt cliffs 'la Falaise du Blot' with the remains of a small chapel built into a crevice in the cliffs. This is the start of a lovely wooded section, with green hills butting in on each bend, little islands, sandy corners, rock ledges, and swimming spots.

Two big bends, and you can see up ahead the impressive medieval village of **Chilhac** which is built on top of a basalt tongue of lava some 100m above the river. The municipal campsite is on the left as you go round the bend - a popular canoeists site, cheap, cheerful, camping naturelle, and a bit scruffy, but with good shade and a café bar. The public landing is on the left downstream from the campsite, before the metal bridge that crosses the river. We recommend a wee foray up to this picturesque laid-back village, take the first turn right after the bridge and head up through the old houses to come out on the ramparts. There's an atmospheric village bar for refreshment that does great omelettes. Also a shop and a boulangerie - whose turn is it to fetch the bread in the morning? - this is a good workout from the campsite if you have a hyperactive member of your group. 2km up the hill south of Chilhac is *'Auberge des Trois Vallées'* - a popular and recommended restaurant.

Continuing on from Chilhac, the river bumbles along for another km to an old mill and weir where there is an entertaining glissière in the centre. Two big bends and 3km brings you in sight of the village of **Lavoûte-Chilhac** which is built around a swan's neck meander in a magnificent setting, with a superb sweep of high old houses accentuating the bend of the river. A great place for photos if you have a support person on the magnificent medieval bridge. Continue around the meander, and under the bridge to land on the left bank some 200m downstream, or a bit further if you want to stay at the campsite.

This is another village that is a must for a stroll, with some fine old medieval buildings and built around the 15th church. Fluffy was pleased to find several ice cream shops, however if you are in need of more substantial refreshment then we can recommend *'le Prieure'* for good cooking and value.

Allier - the village of Lavoûte Chilhac

Lavoûte Chilhac to Brioude	**21 km of class 1-2**	★★	❁❁	☺☺
Water quality - ok	Temperature - warm		Busy? <50	

Lavoûte Chilhac to la Vialette 12km, Vioille Brioude 7km. Brioude campsite 2km.

Summary
This is a popular section offering fine scenery in a green gorge, and pleasant paddling - all straightforward - mainly class 1 with a few slightly harder rapids that add a bit of interest and might possibly be class 2. Although the road is reasonably close, for most of the this run you cannot see it - so it's just you, other paddlers (quite a lot) the river, a green gorge, and the odd heron to follow you down the river.

Shuttle
This is an easy shuttle by road and there is a pleasant cycle shuttle on the right side of the valley if you wish.

Description
Put in at **Lavoûte Chilhac** at the public beach on the downstream side left of the bridge, then for the next 12 km there is only emergency egress from the river. The little commune of Chambon can be seen on the right bank after 4km, followed by a huge ox bow meander. Villeneuve is high up on the left bank after 10km and opposite is the majestic old ruins of St Ilpize Chateau. There is an old weir here which is usually shot on the right. The road bridge is high above the river so there is no easy public access, but you can land below on the beach on the left to shop and explore.

Public access is a lot easier at the campsite in **la Vialette**, which is 2 km further on the left. This is a popular take out for many groups. There's an old mill weir here, which is usually best shot in the middle, and gives a little bit of fun before the fairly straight forward class 1 paddling down to **Vieille Brioude**. Just before the village is a weir on the right and a factory race to the left. The race is impassable so either portage the weir or shoot it - usually on the right. About a km down from the Vieille Brioude road bridge there is a public access point on the left near the Village de Vacances.

One km further, the Senouire river joins from the right (with a fine old 'Roman' bridge just upstream), then there is the **Brioude campsite** *'la Bageasse'* on the left bank (some 4km walk from the town), and a big weir. This is another popular place to **take out** or overnight.

If you want to continue then this weir can be portaged but the river beyond is now shallow and will probably need a lot of frustrating wading. Alternatively it may be possible to run the old mill stream, that goes off left. This may be blocked by trees or other debris and should only be attempted at low water levels. If you do take this stream after 400m it branches and you must take the **right channel.** Towards its end the stream goes under the D588 road through three conduits which terminate in a three short rocky rapids. Inspection, especially for canoeists, is strongly advised. These problems can be by-passed by putting in just below the three conduits at Brioude Canoe Club just off the D588.

Brioude Canoe Club to Cournon **67 km of class 1 (2)** ★ ❁ ☺

Water quality - OK Temperature - warm Busy? <10

Brioude to Brassac les Mines 20km, Issoire 15km, Cournon 32km.

Summary
The river is out of the main Gorges and is now wider and flows in more of a plain, the scenery is still very pleasant and pastoral, with several groups of hills that come close to the river and add distant views. In the second half of the run, from Issoire to Longues, hills encroach on the river and the Allier again flows in more of a gorge with wild, wooded hillsides and a lively current - some guides rate this section as a class 1-2. This makes a nice finale to a river trip and explains why most groups finish at Cournon or Longues.

Shuttle
An easy shuttle by road. If you need it, the driver could return by train from Longues to Brioude.

Description
Best put in is at Brioude Canoe Club just off the D588 (see previous section). From here down to Cournon poses no major problems - pleasant class 1 paddling with only a few weirs, most of which have glissières and give the class (2) suffix. From Brioude to Auzon Bridge is 15km of mainly flat water and then 500m downstream of the bridge is a weir that can normally be shot after inspection. **Brassac les Mines** is a further 4km on the left and has a clean, quiet, cheap campsite that several canoeists have recommended. Mansur Darlington recommends 'for good food go to the restaurant in the car park of the supermarket - don't be put off by the fact that it looks like a glorified shed!'

Another 8km downstream is the next riverside campsite at **Nonette** and a further 7km is **Issoire** together with a canoe club base. Continuing on, it is 20km to **Longues** where just downstream of the bridge is a small weir that can normally be shot left of centre at low summer levels. Another 12km brings you to **Cournon** and the campsite and canoe school 1 km after the bridge on the left bank.

Most paddlers finish their trip here, however it is possible to carry on another 60 km to Vichy, and then a further 100 km to Nevers where the Allier joins the Loire. This lower section has pleasant pastoral scenery but the water quality deteriorates because you are now downstream of Clermont-Ferand. The river flows in a wide valley, giving flat paddling, with a few weirs (mainly shootable). There are few campsites so some wild camping will be needed.

Haut Allier - velo-rail expedition near Pradelles.

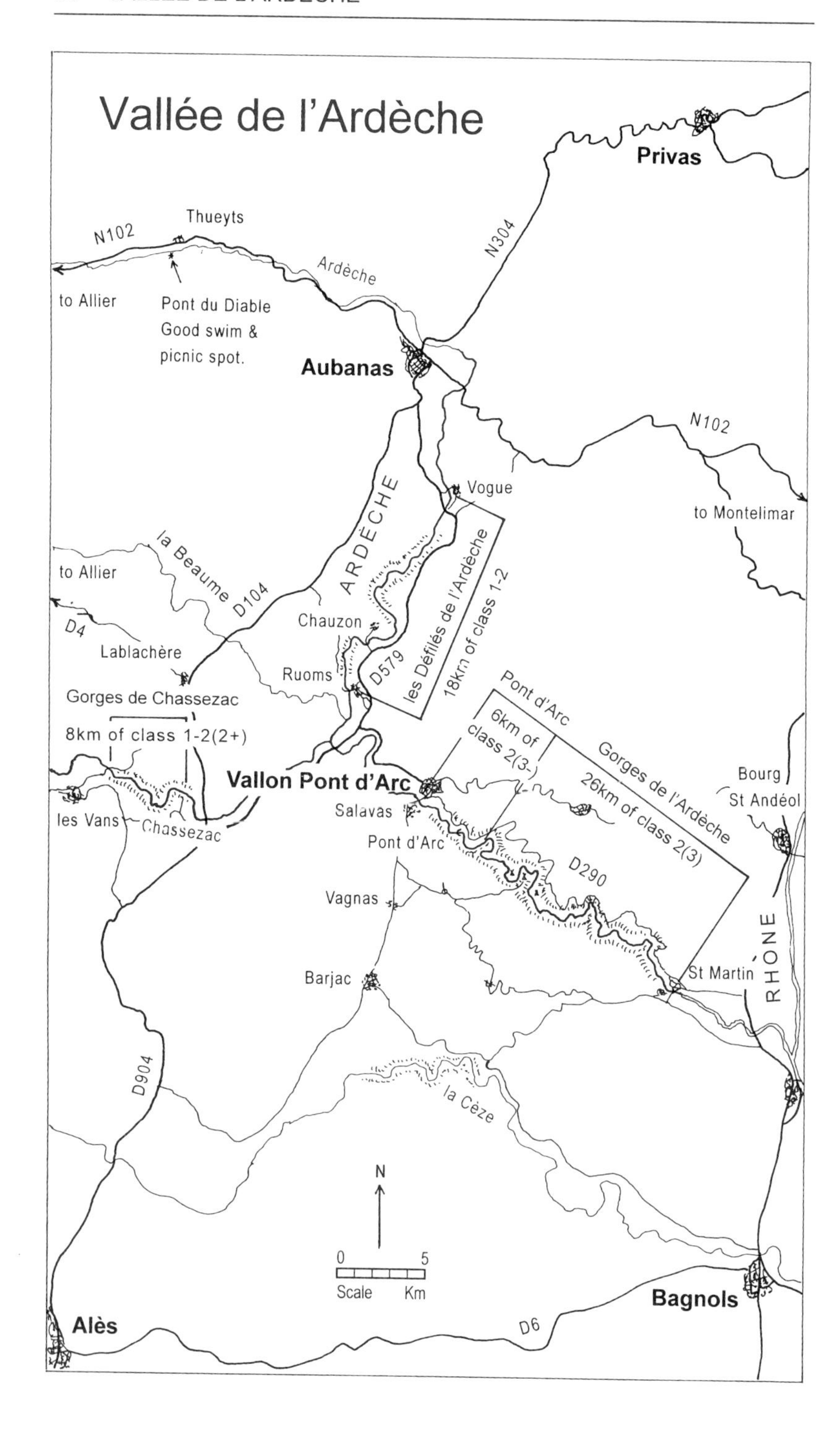
Vallée de l'Ardèche
Privas
Thueyts
N102
N304
Ardèche
to Allier
Pont du Diable
Good swim &
picnic spot.
Aubanas
N102
Vogue
to Montelimar
ARDÈCHE
la Beaume
D104
to Allier
D4
les Défilés de l'Ardèche
18km of class 1-2
Chauzon
Lablachère
D579
Ruoms
Gorges de Chassezac
8km of class 1-2(2+)
Pont d'Arc
6km of
class 2(3-)
Gorges de l'Ardèche
26km of class 2(3)
Vallon Pont d'Arc
Bourg
St Andéol
les Vans
Chassezac
Salavas
Pont d'Arc
D290
Vagnas
RHÔNE
Barjac
St Martin
D904
la Cèze
N
0
5
Scale
Km
Bagnols
Alès
D6

Ardèche

Summary

River and run	Class	Km	Stars	Scen	Fluffy	Busy	Notes
Chassezac Gorges	1-2(2+)	8	★★	❁❁❁	☺☺	<50	Technical paddling, splendid gorge.
Ardèche les Défilés	1-2	18	★	❁❁	☺	<200	Tamer version of the Gorges below
Ardèche - Pont d'Arc	2 (3-)	6	★★	❁❁❁	☺	>200	Foretaste of the Gorges below
Gorges de l'Ardèche	2 (3)	26	★★★	❁❁❁	☺	>200	A world Classic !

The River

The Ardèche Gorges are truly one of the classic canoe trips in Europe with some entertaining rapids in the midst of a magnificent gorge that is now a National Nature Reserve - only spoilt by its very popularity which means that it's crowded in high summer.

The Gorges are the classic stretch, but there is in fact a choice of paddling in this area: only a little way upstream are 'les Défilés de l'Ardèche which are not as grand as the Gorges, so less crowded; also just upstream is the main tributary of the Ardèche, the Chassezac, which has its own highly scenic miniature version of the Gorges de l'Ardèche - again relatively uncrowded. Both of these are ideal for a base and as warm up before doing the Gorges de l'Ardèche..

I first canoed on the Ardèche in 1972 when working as a canoe instructor for PGL, and loved both the job and the area. For many years there was few controls and the river and gorges became more and more crowded and polluted. I, like many people, was put off coming here in high summer because of its reputation.

But, there have been **huge changes in the last 15 years** very much for the better. First and foremost was the creation of a National Nature Reserve and strict controls on camping and litter - the Gorges de l' Ardèche are now back, probably more wild and savage than they were in the 70's. Secondly was the building of two reservoirs upstream to control summer water levels - so now, in summer there is a planned flow of 8 cumecs on the Chassazac, and 12 cumecs on the upper Ardèche giving, in theory, a minimum flow of 20 cumecs down the Gorges. Thirdly there has a big successful effort to build new sewage works and to improve the water quality.

So yes, the Ardèche is crowded and popular, but deservedly so. Don't let any out of date misconceptions put you off coming - do come outside the peak season if you can, but otherwise use this guide to avoid the crowds and make the most of your time here.

Canoe Camping

It is possible to put on at Aubenas and make an 80 km canoe camping trip down the river to finish at the confluence with the Rhone. There are plentiful campsites and this would make a fine out of season 6 day trip. However, most people will probably choose to just paddle the Gorges de l' Ardèche starting at Vallon Pont d'Arc and probably camping one night at a 'bivi' site in the Gorges. Our recommendation if you want to canoe camp the Gorges is to consider doing this as a 3 day, 2 night trip - more details in that section.

Off the river

This is a great area with lots to do and see for the non-paddler. Foremost of these must be the many caves in the area. There's the big spectacular show caves like the ones at Orgnac, that are some of the best in the World - or you can hire a guide and go for your own speleological expedition down a smaller cave. Near Vallon is the recently discovered *'Grotte Chauvet'* which is said to have the best and oldest pre-historic paint cavings in Europe.

The hills and plateaus of the area are excellent for mountain biking, and there are some great walks around the Gorges de l'Ardèche. The road along the north rim of the Gorges is a great tourist panorama and a popular circuit for the road cyclist. There's lots of good bolted climbing cliffs in the area and also some canyonning.

It's worth noting that a popular rough footpath follows the river along the length of the Gorge, fording the river in several places, so it is quite possible for a non-paddler to traverse the gorge at the same time as the rest of the group.

Food and drink

Barjac, the town to the south is probably the place to head to for some good French food at reasonable prices - try *L'Esplanade* here. In la Bastide de Virac, *Le Petite Auberge* has built up a steady reputation over many years. In Vallon, *'ls Queztal'* has been recommended for its Mexican-French food and *'le Point d'Interogation'* for its reasonable value and interior ambience. The *'Café du Nord'* in Vallon and *'le Chardon'* in Vagnas are typical traditional friendly bars, popular with paddlers and where the patrons speak English.

Camping

There are a huge number of sites in this area, most with excellent facilities but a wide variation in price and popularity. We recommend that in high summer you avoid the crowded riverside sites close to Vallon. Instead, for a riverside site we suggest that you base yourself on the Chassezac or les Defiles de l'Ardèche - we have listed sites there under these headings.

Le Mas de Serret is out in the wilds, roughly half way down the river on the edge of the gorge, so is a convenient base if you don't want to canoe camp, tel: 04 75 38 60 93. The Municipal site at Orgnac, tel: 04 75 38 63 68, and *'Rouviere le Pins'* at Vagnas, tel: 04 75 38 61 41, both have swimming pools and can be recommended for families.

There are some excellent Gites in the area - we recommend the *'Domaine de l'Astic'* an ancient manor house, now converted into comfortable *** gites, perched high on a ridge with its own private swimming pool : wwwdomaine-lastic.fr.

Maps and Guides

IGN TOP100 sheet 59 covers the whole of this area at a scale of 1:100,000, but the IGN TOP25 sheet 2939OT 'Gorges de l'Ardèche' is the best buy for walking and mountain biking. If you are planning a descent of the Gorges then we recommend the full colour waterproof map *'Plan Guide les Gorges de l'Ardèche'* - this has an amazing amount of detail - shows all the rapids, beaches, springs, paths, caves, etc. There is a similar map for the upper river - *'Plan Guide des Defiles'*.

There is a fine little book called *'Rivières d'Ardèche'* by World Champion Claude Peschier - this covers all the rivers of the area, but published in 1987.

Fluffy on cultural research.

Claude Peschier has also produced more of a coffee table book - *'Eaux Vives d'Ardèche'* that would make a fine souvenir of your stay. A more modern guide, 1994, is the *Zoom Guide* by Jean-Michel Metzger that gives ideas for canyoning, canoeing, climbing, walks, and mountain bike routes.

These maps and guides are available from local book shops or by mail order from le Canotier.

Tourist Offices - www.ardeche-guide.com

Aubenas - tel: 04 75 89 02 03
les Vans - tel: 04 75 37 24 48
Ruoms - tel: 04 75 93 91 90 www.ot.ruoms@bigfoot.com
Vallon Pont d'Arc - tel: 04 75 88 04 01 www.vallon-pont-darc.com
St Martin - tel: 04 75 98 70 91

Canoe Hire and rafting

Something like 40 companies offer canoe hire - please consult local tourist offices for an up-to-date list. *Alpha Bateaux* is an example of one well-established large operator, tel: 04 75 88 08 29., www canoe-france.com.

Several people have recommended *Alain Bateaux* if you want an English speaking local river guide to make all the arrangements and lead your group down the river - tel: 04 75 37 17 22.

A Pirate to the Rescue

There's a certain ghoulish delight in stopping at rapids like 'la Dent Noir' to watch the carnage and wonder at how stupid we humans can be at times. We were making lunch here one day when a big Klepper kayak shot the rapid, husband and wife paddling, with a baby tied in with a length of rope - we watched in horror as it broached broadside on the infamous Black Tooth. One of our instructors was cutting bread at the time, and quick as flash, like a pirate, dived into the river with the bread knife between his teeth and cut the baby loose.

Nature Reserve Regulations

- No rafts or inflatable boats for more than 3 people.
- Buoyancy Aids must be worn when canoeing.
- No children under 7 years of age.
- No entry into the Reserve after 1600 hours.
- People must arrive and book in 'les Bivi' campsites before 1800 hours.
- No wild camping.
- Leave nothing but footprints.

Other rivers

If you are here early season then there's some good white water kayaking in the area when rivers like the Beaume and the upper Chassezac are running. To the south, the Cèze and Gardon offer easy open canoeing in early summer, and to the east of the Rhone the **Drome** is another river popular for canoe touring. None of these rivers can be assured of having sufficient water in July and August so we recommend the Allier as the nearest river in this guide - approximately two hours drive north west.

Les Bateliers de l'Ardèche

Most people wouldn't think of the Gorges de l'Ardèche as a waterway and navigation for the transport of people and goods, but despite its rapids, in the centuries before there were roads, the river, represented an easier and cheaper way of transporting goods than by pack horse or mule trains over the rough paths of the plateau. The Bateliers (Boatmen) used very similar boats to the ones they use today for carrying tourists, a flat bottomed punt, which they would pole down the river.

Coming back upstream would have been much harder work and most probably this would have been with an empty boat that would have been lined or tracked up many of the rapids. Apparently there were fixed chains in some spots next to cliffs and ledges where the boats could be hauled up hand over hand. In historical times, the river was also used (like many other rivers in Europe) for floating down rafts of logs which would be used for things like ship building.

In the 19th century tourists started coming to the see the famous sites of the Gorges de l'Ardèche and the Bateliers then started a thriving business taking visitors down through the gorges. This became even more popular as roads improved and more tourists arrived by charabanc. The better roads and the motor car meant that the boats could be trailed back to the top of the Gorges behind the local taxi.

The Bateliers still offer a highly skilled service on the river for the less active tourist who wants a safe and relaxed journey down through the Gorges de l'Ardèche - please contact the tourist office for further details.

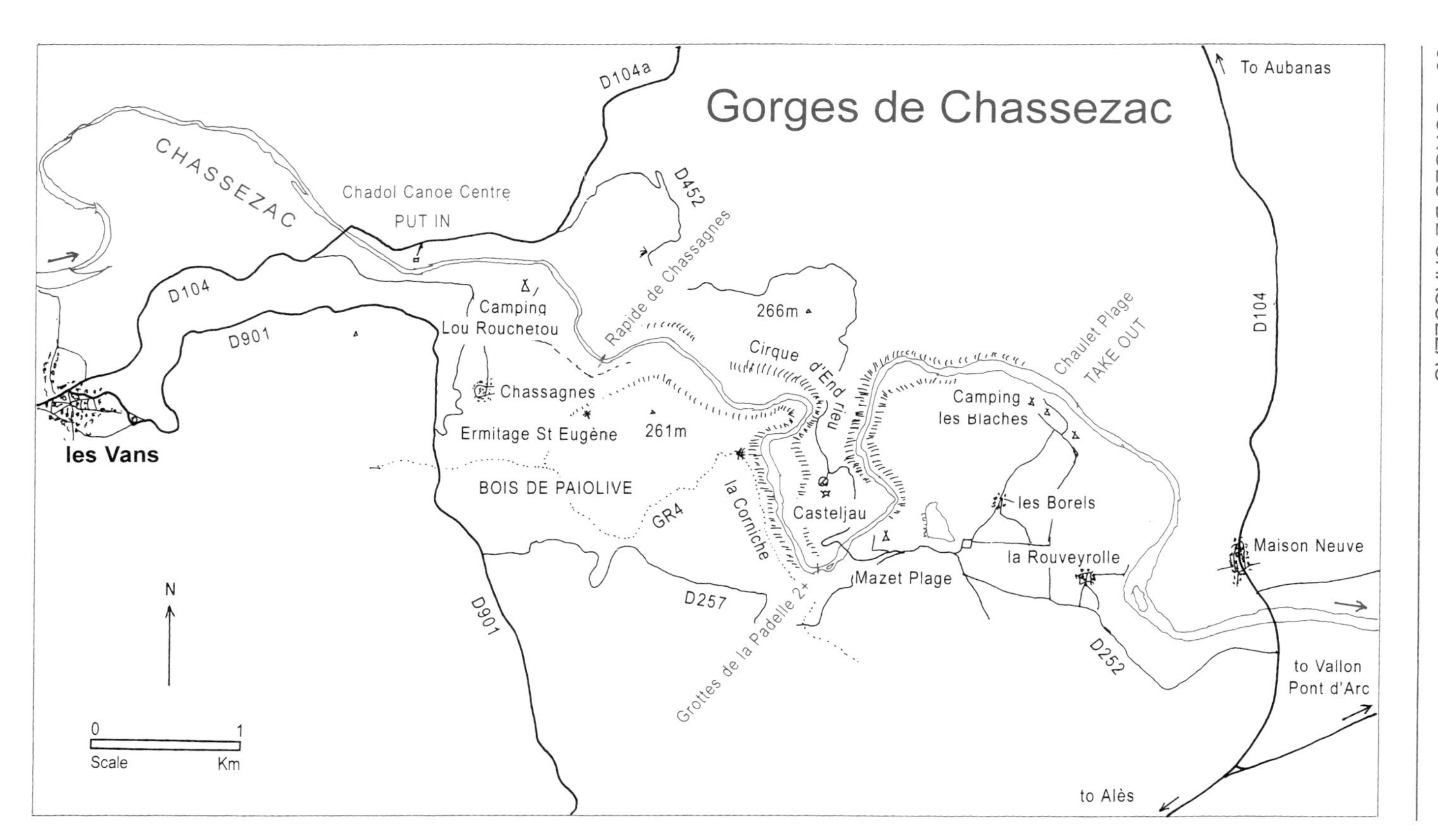
Gorges de Chassezac
To Aubanas
D104a
CHASSEZAC
Chadol Canoe Centre
PUT IN
D452
Rapide de Chassagnes
D104
Camping
Lou Rouchetou
D901
266m
Cirque d'End rieu
Chaulet Plage
TAKE OUT
D104
Chassagnes
Camping
les Blaches
Ermitage St Eugène
261m
les Vans
BOIS DE PAIOLIVE
les Borels
GR4
la Corniche
Casteljau
Maison Neuve
la Rouveyrolle
Mazet Plage
N
D257
D901
Grottes de la Padelle 2+
D252
to Vallon
Pont d'Arc
0
1
Scale
Km
to Alès

Gorges du Chassezac - **8 km of class 1-2 (2+)** ★★ ❁❁❁ ☺☺

Water quality - good Temperature - warm Busy? <50

Pont de Fer to Mazet Plage 5km, Chaulet Plage 3km.

Summary

The Chassezac is the main tributary of the Ardèche and cuts through a range of limestone hills to create a fine little gorge - something like a mini-Gorges de l'Ardèche' with cliffs soaring some 120m. The water is constrained by cliffs and bedrock ledges, with some quite technical class 2 rapids, making this a run that is a bit difficult for the complete beginner and we saw relatively few hire boats. For the paddler with a little experience, this is a fun run and very satisfying to work out the best lines down the rapids.

The river receives a guaranteed flow from the reservoirs in the mountains upstream - and indeed you are close to the mountains here, and only some 25km from the source of the Tarn on 1699m Mont du Lozère - worth a scenic drive maybe. The Chassezac gorges are also popular with rock climbers with many bolted routes on the cliffs rising from the river. A special hazard is falling climbers.

Camping and Shuttle

Les Vans is a small town with most shops and services, but above the river and some 2km from the put in. The shuttle is short, and although it needs a climb of 100m, it's a pleasant and scenic ride if you need to do it by bike - most scenic on the north bank. *'Lou Rouchetou'* tel: 04 75 37 33 13, is a green shady campsite on the right bank near the put-in. *'Mazet Plage'* campsite tel: 04 75 39 32 56, is approximately half way down and then there are several campsites at the end of the Gorges - *'Camping les Blaches'* tel: 04 75 39 05 26 was a bit wilder than the others and would probably suit canoeists more.

To drive to the take-out, follow signs to **'Chaulet Plage'** where there is a couple of restaurants and bars next to the beach - drive past these and a track goes down to the beach itself. If you have the time, we recommend a walk look around the 'Bois de Paiolive' which is an area of Karst limestone carved by rain and erosion into fantastic shapes and sculptures.

Description

Put in 200m downstream from *le Pont de Fer* at the **'Chadol Canoe Centre'**. A sign here says 'Canoeists Welcome' - there's a restaurant, bar, ice creams, toilets, etc. For the first 2 km the river is quite wide with 3 or 4 small rapids running over gravel bars. We paddled this river in low water, but even so, didn't need to wade anything.

The hills close into the river and some rock ledges on the right up ahead mark the *'Grotte de Fromentin'* cave, and the start of the gorge. This is a local picnic and swimming spot. The current runs into water-worn smooth ledges on the right, and has created the *'Rapide de Chassagnes'*, a surf wave, and a good swimming spot.

Training for the Orinoco

John Wilde had told us about the upper Chassezac and that it was a 'really great paddle'. I suppose we should have thought about it a little - a recommendation from the Wilde Man was always an unknown. Anyway, Mike Jones (Leader of the 'Canoeing Down Everest' Expediton), Pete Midwood and I, plus various other cookies and swampies who were working with us at PGL squashed ourselves into Mike's Toyota and my battered Anglia van and off we set into the hills.

We all had hangovers, Mike in particular, an occupational hazard of working for PGL on the Ardèche. John Wilde said he couldn't make the trip. Eventually we arrived at the put in - a small village by the dam. We looked over the parapet: the river was dry. Wilde Man's assurance that the dam released on Wednesdays was obviously incorrect. We retired somewhat relieved to the bar - none of us really felt like paddling and the alternative of a liquid lunch, a game of boule, a stroll, and a cruise back to PGL in the evening seemed a much better plan.

About an hour later in the bar one of the locals asked if we were going for a paddle. *"Non il n'y a pas du l'eau"* (No there's no water.) *"Ah, mais maintenant, il y a du l'eau, le barrage est ouvert"* Oh shit! Full of confidence and vin rouge we felt duty bound to set off for the river. Bravado and chaos were evenly mixed - Mike discovered he had no shoes to paddle with and so ended up duct taping a pair of old flip-flops to his feet. A pick up point was loosely arranged for the drivers to find us - "next bridge down wherever that is" was about the extent of the agreement.

I launched and hit the first hole about 50 metres downstream. The boat performed a fast and violent back-ender and then ended up surfing in the hole. Soon I was swimming. Pride was hurt but nothing else, so I rescued my boat and paddle and the three of us set off again a little more circumspectly. Soon Pete Midwood was swimming for some other reason. This really was not looking good - this was supposed to be a training trip for our British Kayak Expedition to the Orinocco - the follow up to our famous 'Canoeing Down Everest' trip of the year before!

Three months of guiding groups of school kids down the Ardèche in open canoes had obviously not been the right kind of training for we highly tuned athletes - two thirds of the team members swimming on an unknown, innocuous river in southern France! Oh well - we gathered together Pete's gear and apprehensively paddled on. We were relieved that from then on things got easier, there were no more mishaps and wonder of wonder, the cars were even at the first bridge downstream. Was it coincidence, that when we got back home to Vagnas, John Wilde had left for an international slalom?

Dave Manby

On the left ahead are the curving limestone cliffs of the *Cirque d'Endrieu*, and the next 3km are beautifully wild and scenic, with cliffs, rocks, wooded slopes, a wild river flowing over boulder rapids, and very few people. A red kite circled overhead and we were amazed and delighted how quiet it was. At the end of this 3km stretch look out for a sharp left bend - this marks where the *'Grottes de la Padelle'* rapid flows into a dangerous looking undercut on the right - there is usually a safe shoot on the left. The bridge and **Mazet Plage** campsite are just downstream.

Some 500m downstream the river takes a sharp left bend and a big yellow sign on the right says *'Danger d'Aspiration'*, presumably more for the benefit of swimmers. The river flows in a tight gorge with sheer rock walls some 80m high on both sides - a popular climbing venue - and a few gentle class 1 rapids. 2km round the long right hand bend and the river comes out of the gorge, the valley widens, the river becomes shallow, and a broken weir marks the take out and the welcoming ice cream café at **Chaulet Plage**, on the right.

The valley is flat below here, the river widens out and shallow rapids may require wading - making it an un-inspiring 13km of 'dog water' to the confluence with the Ardèche and a further 5km to Vallon.

Gorges du Chassezac - surfing on the 'Rapide de Chassagnes' *Ray Goodwin*

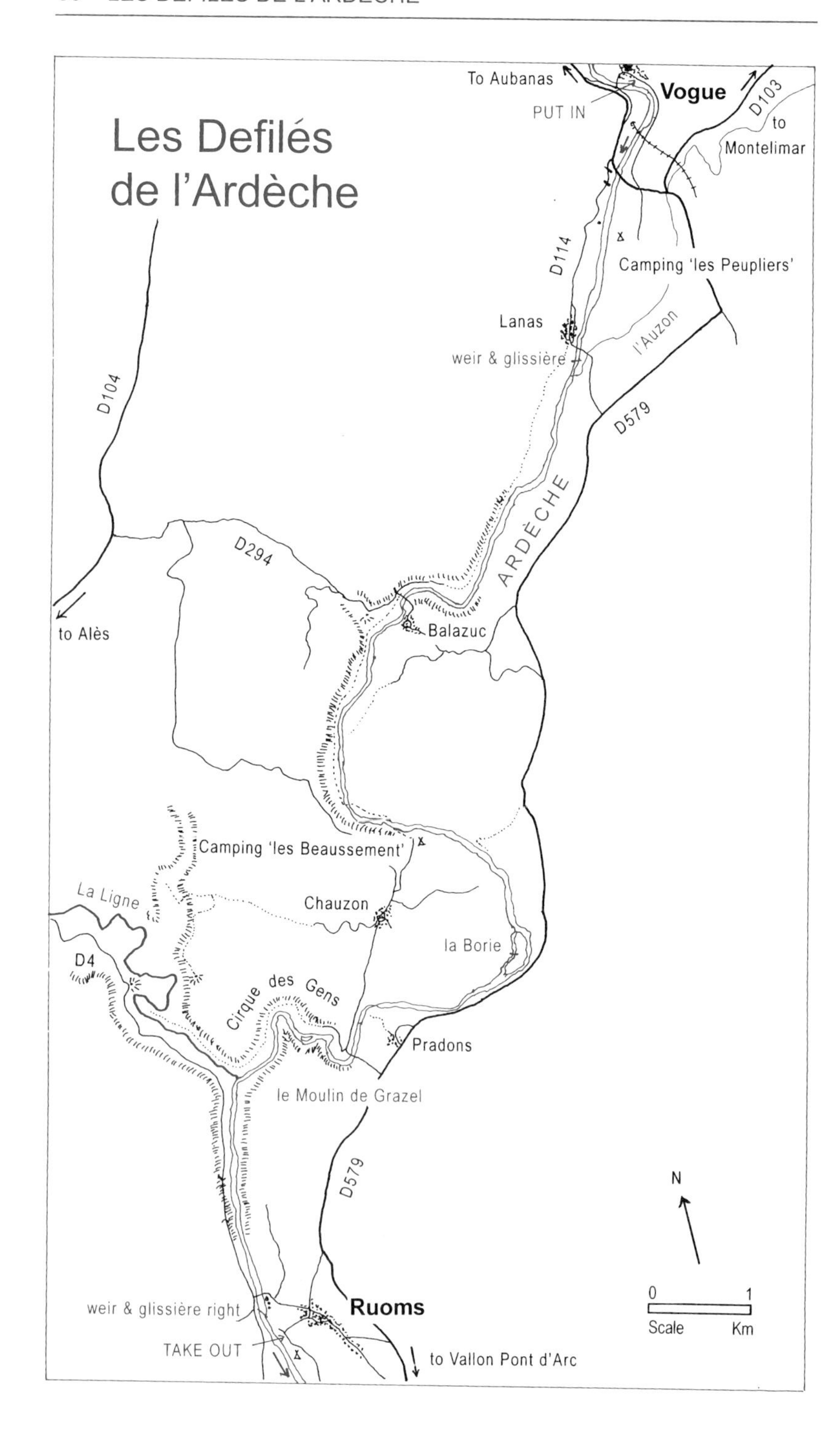
Les Defilés de l'Ardèche
To Aubanas
PUT IN
Vogue
D103
to Montelimar
D114
Camping 'les Peupliers'
Lanas
weir & glissière
l'Auzon
D579
D104
ARDÈCHE
D294
to Alès
Balazuc
Camping 'les Beaussement'
La Ligne
Chauzon
la Borie
D4
Cirque des Gens
Pradons
le Moulin de Grazel
D579
N
0
1
Scale
Km
weir & glissière right
Ruoms
TAKE OUT
to Vallon Pont d'Arc

les Défilés de l'Ardèche	**18 km of class 1-2**	★	❁❁	☺
Water quality - OK.	Temperature - warm		Busy? <200	

Vogue to Balazuc 7km, Camping 'les Beaussement' 3km, Ruoms 8km.

Summary

A friendly and easier alternative to its big brother down stream, les Défilés is another gorge, less dramatic, and not as wild. The river has less current, with shallow rapids that are mainly class 1, with a few class 2. In high summer, the flow is supposed to be a minimum of 12 cumecs, but we reckoned it was more like 8 cumecs when we did it. This section has some picturesque old villages to explore and is also not as crowded so it makes an ideal warm up before doing les Gorges de l'Ardèche, and it is also an ideal base for exploring the area.

We recommend the section between Vogue and Ruoms as the best section for paddling. Further upstream, from Aubenas to Vogue is a fine bouncy class 3 paddle in early summer or at other times when water levels are sufficient and is popular for rafting in higher water. From Ruoms down to Vallon Pont d'Arc is pretty flat and boring, with wide, shallow class 1 rapids, that will often need wading.

Ruoms is a small town with most shops and services. The old villages of Vogue, and Balazuc are very picturesque and well worth a stroll, particularly when it is quieter in early evening, with the setting sun glowing on the warm stone building. There are some excellent walks along the cliffs with river panoramas.

Camping and Shuttle

The take out at **Ruoms** is downstream of the town on the left bank. Follow the signs to 'Plage' and 'camping'. The shuttle is fast and easy by vehicle, along the D579, which is a busy road so not ideal for cycling. There are no other alternative practical routes but note that this is a popular section with commercial operators so you should be able to negotiate a seat in a mini bus. Put in at the beach on the left bank at Vogue were there is plenty of parking.

There are a dozen or so riverside campsites on this section. We stayed, and can recommend *'Camping Beaussement'* at **Chauzon**, - a shady old orchard which was popular with canoeists, and made a good base for exploring the area. tel: 04 75 39 72 06, email beaussement@wanadoo.fr.

At **Vogue** you might like to consider: *'les Peupliers'* tel: 04 75 37 71 47, email:camping.peupliers07@wanadoo.fr. *'Domaine du Cros d'Auzon'* tel: 04 75 37 75 86, email: croz.d.auzon@wanadoo.fr.

At Ruoms, near the take out is: 'Camping Municipal' tel: 04 75 93 99 16. On the opposite bank, 1km down river is *'le Peyroche'* tel: 04 75 39 79 39.

Description

The ancient village of **Vogue** has a huge, magnificent old chateau, so this is a pleasant place to explore if you have time whilst waiting for a shuttle. For the first 3km the river is quite wide - there are easy rapids over stone and gravel bars and in low water some wading may be needed. These lead you down underneath the old railway viaduct and the high road bridge. *'Les Peupliers'* campsite is on the left and another km brings you to the road bridge, high over the river, which leads to **Lanas** village on the right - there is a public beach and landing on the right below the bridge if you want to go and explore.

Some 600m downstream of Lanas bridge is a low weir with a **glissière** in the middle - a straight-forward, but fun shoot. Just downstream is a 'little Amazon' - the river changes character with narrow channels fringed with green vegetation and over-hanging trees. Then 500m further around a curving bend, it opens out again and there are long lines of low cliffs on the right, one on top of the other, like long rows of steps. The *'Grotte de Estinettes'* rapid is at the start of these cliffs - keep left of centre to avoid the undercuts on the right.

This is the real start to les Défilés, with a series of class 2 rapids taking you around the bend, with long lines of limestone cliffs on both banks forming a miniature Grand Canyon - only some 80m high, but still wild grandeur. The rapids have some big boulders in them, fallen from the cliffs above, so some well defined eddies and a few small play waves. Beware of what the French call a 'drossage' where the current sweeps you into the cliff face on the outside of bends.

Around the bend is the road bridge and old village of **Balazuc**, classified as one of the 'most beautiful old villages of France'. We suggest landing here to explore - there's a public landing place at the beach on the left with parking, a bar and ice creams. Probably the most scenic 3 km of the Défilés starts here with easy, but technical rapids to provide entertainment as you travel down the gorge with long lines of cliffs on both sides. *'Le Beaussement'* campsite is on the right at the end of the cliffs and there is a public landing here, with a lane that leads up to **Chauzon**.

The river widens out for the next 3 km around the big bend, with a lot of 'bump and scrape' easy rapids. Keep a look out for **'la Borie'**, a hard class 2 rapid, which is when you can see cliffs ahead on the left. There is a big conglomerate rock in the middle of the rapid and old bridge pier on an island in the river, towards which the current sweeps. Avoid the left hand channel that is often blocked by trees and if in doubt land and inspect on the right.

2km on, the river bends left and on the left is a beach and public access to the little village of les **Pradons**. There are cliffs on the right and then the high road bridge. Just downstream of the bridge on the right is a private beach, pedalos, and snack bar. Then 300m round the left hand bend is the remains of the old *Mill 'le Moulin de Grazel'* and the start of about 5 good technical class 2 rapids as the river bends first one way, then another, through the spectacular *Cirque de Gens*. There are impressive cliffs, 'beaumes' on both sides and then a side valley, the **'Défilé de la Lignne'** joins from the right.

Long lines of cliffs continue into the distance, so vertical and close to the river that the road has to be tunnelled out as an over-hanging ledge on the right. Then the cliffs end, the bridge can be seen in the distance, the river widens, the current slows and you have a sense of anti-climax as you paddle out of the Gorges and towards the town of **Ruoms**. But waiting downstream of the bridge is a stunning finale - a sinuous, long, high, glissière that shoots you down the right hand side of the weir - great fun and very photogenic. **Take out** 200m below at the public beach for celebration ice creams.

The river widens beyond here and the next 13 km to Vallon Pont d'Arc is pretty flat, shallow, and uninspiring, so we suggest you give this section a miss unless you are camping en route, or doing a longer tour. It does however, have a few class one rapids, and the 4 weirs have glissières so there is some fun to be had!

Gorges de l'Ardèche - looking down at 'le Gaud' bivi-site,
Photo taken at lunch-time in peak season - despite this, notice how the river is relatively un-crowded because the 'daily wave' of canoes has passed by.

Ardèche - Pont d'Arc	**6 km of class 2 (3-)**	★★	❁❁❁	☺
Water quality - o.k.	Temperature - warm		Busy? >200	

Vallon to Pont d'Arc 4km, to Chames 2km.

Summary

French canoe hire operators call this 'le Mini-Descent' it's really the first 6km of the normal trip down the Gorges de l'Ardèche, - an aperitif of good things to come: oustanding scenery and fun white water. It has road access, and includes the famous 'Pont d'Arc' so it's well worth thinking of doing this as a separate trip if you have the time. It is a popular run and gets very busy so it is best to do this when it is quieter, preferably as a **leisurely evening run**, when you should have the river pretty much to yourselves. Most two day trips down the Gorges start in the morning around 9 a.m. so a run in the afternoon, or at lunch time (sacre bleu - what a terrible idea!) will be quieter. You could thoeretically hammer down this section in half an hour, but we suggest allowing 2-3 hours to saviour and enjoy this wonderful run.

Camping and Shuttle

Camping next to the river near Pont d'Arc is a very special location and has many logistical advantages so the sites command a premium price, are very crowded, and it is essential to book in high season. In our opinion the five sites downstream of the Arc near **Chames** are the best sited: *'Pont d'Arc'* tel: 04 75 88 00 64, *'Tourre'* tel: 04 75 88 00 11, *'du Midi'* tel: 04 75 88 06 78, *'la Rouviere'* tel: 04 75 37 10 07, and *'Camp des Gorges'* tel: 04 75 88 00 05.

The shuttle is straight forward, along the busy minor road that follows the valley. If you have plenty of time, you could return to Vallon along the adventurous footpath on the river right bank. The take out and parking area at Chames is sign posted off the road (You may have to pay for parking)

Description

Put in at the public beach at the Municipal campsite *'Camping Zamenhof'* on the river right just downstream of the bridge. The first 2km are easy paddling with a wide shallow river and some 3 class 1 rapids - in low water the problem is picking out where the main current runs so that you don't go aground. There are numerous campsites on both banks, and lots of people wading and swimming.

The roped off bathing area of *'les Tunnels'* campsite marks the start of the Gorges and the road can be seen cut out of the cliffs high above the river on the left. The river bends right here and there is the first rapid of note **'Rapide du Cayre-Crest'**. This is best run on the right, close to the huge house rock near the beach - at some levels and in some years, the only shoot is centre left and then the current can project you into the rock face, and a near certain capsize.

English groups used to know this house rock as *'Post Office Rock'* and it has always been a favourite spot for swimming, climbing and jumping - (check the water for hidden rocks). It has hosted numerous mad games and escapades - we used to take the smallest member of the group, wrap him in about 20 buoyancy aids then roll him off the top!. The cliffs now start on the right and there is a wonderful sculptured rock ledge on the right with a spring about 150m after 'Post Office Rock'.

érault - 'le Moulin' rapid below Ganges. Alain Nicolet

Tarn - the ‘Monsters’ shooting the glissière at les Vignes.

ıffy goes caving. Kate Banks

Orb - below Tarassac.

If you hug the cliffs on the right you end up in a cul-de-sac and a huge overhang which makes a super cool shady spot for lunch - if some noisy youth group hasn't already bagged it. (the warm, still water at the end is also a favourite spot for water snakes).

This is probably a good spot to land anyway, because you have two noteworthy rapids in the next 400m that you will probably want to inspect. The first one **'la Ribeige'** has a rib of rock that has acquired magical magnetic properties for attracting plastic boats, but is normally straight forward once you have inspected and checked out the line. 300m downstream is the lead in to **'le Charlemagne'** which again is much easier once you have looked at it. Most English groups call this simply ***'Pont d'Arc rapid'*** because the arch can be seen in the background downstream.

The lead up to the rapid has about 200m of a rocky channel, and you need to keep centre-right all the way. (In low water, commercial groups like PGL normally station instructors on the main rocks, so that if one of their boats goes off course they can quietly and casually give it a discrete nudge down the main channel - a supreme example of how to combine maximum customer fulfilment with optimum safety). The final drop forms a big wave that is highly photogenic so it's well worth someone setting up here to take photographs. In the event of a capsize, its flat water below - with a large busy swimming beach on the left, and there is plenty of time to recover boats and people. The wave is normally excellent for surfing, but the problem is the huge number of passing boats - as much as 300 an hour!

Below the rapid, the river is flat for some 500m, up to, leading under, and downstream of the famous **Pont d'Arc** - so take your time, drift along, look up and around and saviour this fantastic 60m high natural rock arch. For the experienced climber, it is possible (but not recommended) to climb the arch (see inset box) or to scramble into one of the caves and surprise your friends by jumping out of one of the 'maggot holes' in the rock wall on the right. We suggest landing on the pebble beach on the right below to play and explore, although Fluffy quite naturally prefers the left hand beach where there is an ice cream shop.

Setting off again - a super cool seal launch off the pebble beach at its upstream end - there's a straight forward class one rapid just round the corner and then a fast current which takes you for the next 2km around a long bend with sheer rock ledges and cliffs on the right and pebbly beaches and campsites on the left. Another class one rapid follows with a few clean eddy lines on the right that the cognoscenti can use for play moves. Note how clear and clean the water is, and count the fish!

'Camp des Gorges' is the last of the campsites and then the public landing and take out point is on the left after another 500m. Don't miss this because its the last road access for some 30km. However don't panic if you do, as it's in fact easy to wade back upstream on the river right.

A really deviant idea if you have time on your hands, want a bit more white water fun, have a light boat, and don't mind a 20 inute portage is to carry on around the great loop of river that is ahead, run two good rapids - *'la Ravaou' and 'les Trois Eaux'* and then carry back over the narrow neck of the bend -*'le Pas du Mousse'*.

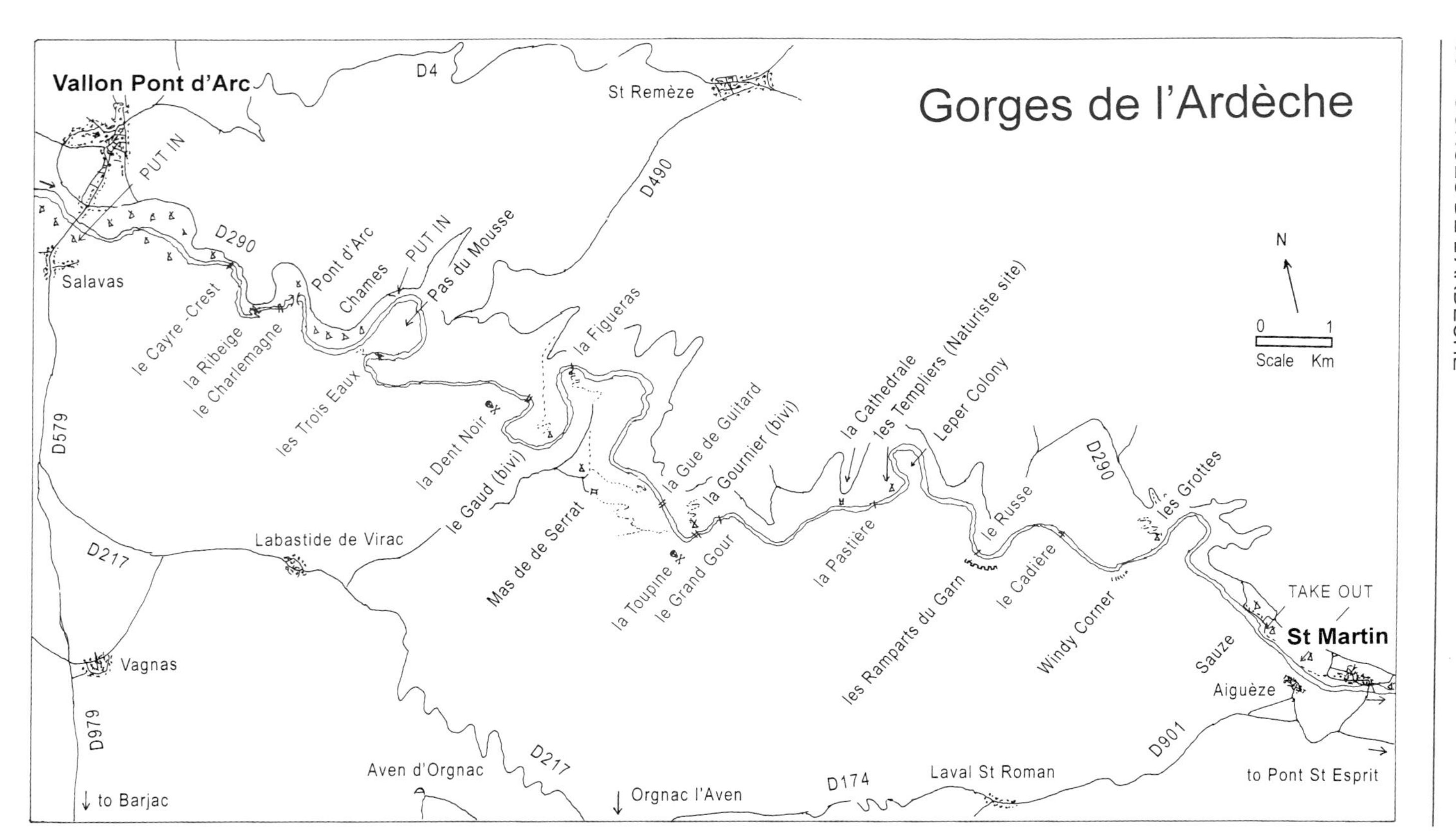

Gorges de l'Ardèche
Vallon Pont d'Arc
D4
St Remèze
PUT IN
D490
D290
Salavas
Pont d'Arc
Chames
PUT IN
Pas du Mousse
le Cayre -Crest
la Ribeige
le Charlemagne
les Trois Eaux
la Figueras
la Dent Noir
le Gaud (bivi)
Mas de de Serrat
la Gue de Guitard
la Gournier (bivi)
la Toupine
le Grand Gour
la Cathedrale
les Templiers (Naturiste site)
Leper Colony
la Pastière
les Ramparts du Garn
le Russe
le Cadière
Windy Corner
D290
les Grottes
N
0
1
Scale Km
TAKE OUT
St Martin
Sauze
Aiguèze
D579
D217
Labastide de Virac
Vagnas
D979
to Barjac
Aven d'Orgnac
D217
Orgnac l'Aven
D174
Laval St Roman
D901
to Pont St Esprit

Gorges de l'Ardèche	26 km of class 2 (3)	★★★	❁❁❁	☺
Water quality - o.k.	Temperature - warm		Busy? >200	

Chames to Gaud 7km, Gournier 5km, St Martin 14km.

Summary

Outstanding scenery and great paddling in one of the most beautiful gorges in Europe. But very popular and crowded in summer, **especially at weekends**. Local experts reckon that daily numbers paddling the Gorges de l'Ardèche in high summer are actually now a little less than they were five years ago, as people have been put off by the crowds. Our advice is to ignore any wild tales you may have heard and to use the advice in this section to plan your trip so that you avoid the crowds and have a magnificent trip.

Camping

See the notes in the main section on where to establish a base camp if you are in the area for several days - it obviously depends on factors like how many in your group, how long you want to stay in the area, how you plan to do your shuttle, etc. Logistically, if you are only here for a few nights, it probably makes most sense to camp near Chames, at the put in, or at 'le Mas de Serret', half way down the Gorges. You may want to consider camping at St Martin at the end of the trip - *'Camping les Gorges'* is probably the most convenient site here, almost next to the river at Sauze, 2km upstream - tel: 04 75 04 61 09.

Camping in the Gorges

It's possible to paddle all the Gorges as a long day - but it is a long hard day that we do not recommend - these are magnificent gorges and even for an experienced paddler, to blast through as some kind of endurance epic is just madness. Much, much better is to carry lightweight camping gear with you and make an overnight 'bivi' camp deep in the gorges - this then becomes a mini-expedition and deeply satisfying!

This is in fact quite easy because the creation of the Reserve Naturelle established two official 'bivi' campsites in the Gorges, which are in fact fully equipped campsites with toilets, showers, barbecue stands (and free charcoal), together with first aid and emergency evacuation if necessary. You can only stay in these a maximum of two nights and you must buy and pre-book a ticket at the Reserve office in Vallon (next to the Tourist Information Office). You must arrive before 1800 hours and each site has a maximum of 600 people so they can get crowded and noisy. The second one *'la Gournier'* is nearer the half way point so tends to be busier. Note that wild camping in the Gorges is strictly forbidden - the Gendarmerie operate river, foot, and helicopter patrols and fines can be 135 euros per person.

An alternative to camping in these bivi sites is to hike out to the top of the gorges at the half way point, *'le Mas de Serret'* and camp here - you don't want to have to carry all your camping gear up 600m so it is best to set up a base and camp here before your descent (note to take stout trainers - the path is rough, steep and requires care).

The Shuttle

If you are hiring your canoes and gear from a local operator then they will deliver you back to the start point or your campsite, so it is all easy logistics, and good value, however you may be limited in your departure and collection times so that you end up going down the river in the main wave of canoes.

If you have your own boats, then you will have the problem of getting your vehicle shuttled to the end of the river at St Martin. Operators will happily sell you spare seats in their buses for the return journey back from St Martin - ideal for the drivers, but they don't want to know about transporting private boats. Taxi firms normally have roof racks and can take one or two boats and are well worth considering. You are looking at a 30km journey which is not going to be cheap, but if you look at the cost and hassle of perhaps two double shuttles it's probably well worth it. Last time I did the Gorges we finished at St Martin at around 7 p.m. with the river to ourselves, piled into the local restaurant for a well earned dinner and wine, and phoned up for a taxi to take us (most of us sleeping) back to our campsite - a perfect way to end the trip.

Security is not a big problem in the Gorges, but you might like to take a cable lock so that you can lock your boats together when you leave them overnight. We recommend that you keep paddles and gear with you, and make sure you pull your boats at least 2m vertically above river level, in case of sudden overnight flood.

How to beat the crowds

On most days in the summer a great plastic wave of canoes sets off from Chames at 0900 every morning. On Saturday and Sundays in July this can be over 2000 people. This can a great experience, but perhaps not quite how you meant it! Neither is it just one big wave of canoes - because there is another 2 day wave that sets off from the Bivi sites each morning at around 0900. All these waves tend to come together in the last few hours of the afternoon from 1500 to 1700 on the final stretch to St Martin. But outside these waves the river can be surprisingly quiet - for example at St Martin at noon there will only be maybe 20 boats in sight, at 1600 it's bank to bank plastic. Look down into the middle of the gorge from one of the viewpoints at 0900 or 1700 and you will see only a handful of boats if any at all. So it's not really difficult to miss the crowds. We recommend:

1. If possible, come outside Peak season - before mid-July or after 14th Aug.
2. Try to avoid a trip at weekends.
3. If you hire gear, then try and arrange non-standard times.
4. Spread your trip over several days.
5. Book your trip on a rainy day!
6. Try and paddle outside the main waves - see below for a few ideas:

Plan A Establish camp at Le Mas de Serret. Day 1, have an afternoon paddle down to Chames, Day 2, shuttle one car to St Martin in the morning, then set off after lunch from Chames for an afternoon and evening paddle down to Le Mas de Serrat. Day 2 - Make a leisurely start to arrive down at St Martin in early evening around 1900, after most tourists are off the river (most pick ups are around 1700). Load your boats on your shuttle car and go for a celebration meal, then back to le Mas campsite. If necessary hire a taxi to take extra people.

Plan B. Camp at one of the riverside sites near Chames. Day 1 arrive and book in at the site, buy tickets for le Bivi, then afternoon paddle down from Vallon to the site, evening try and pre-pack and get organised. Day 2, early start on the river to beat the 0900 wave and arrive at Le Gournier bivi site early afternoon and hopefully the pick of the best sites. Day 3, early start to again beat the rush and arrive down at St Martin for early afternoon. Driver hitches back to Vallon to pick up the car whilst rest of team explore Aigueze, swim and picnic, or you could set up camp at one of the St Martin campsites - alternatively, If you have hired gear from an operator then they will run you back around 1700 to Vallon or your campsite, and its all a lot easier.

Plan C Much the same as Plan B, but you build in an extra day camping and playing at Pont d'Arc after Day 1, so the driver can do a car shuttle from Vallon to St Martin and then come back on a bus at 1700 to the campsite. So on Day 4 your car is waiting for you at St Martin and it doesn't matter when you arrive.

Several people have suggested that the Gorges are such a great place to be, that there is a lot to be said for camping at both bivi sites, to give you time to explore and relax in the Gorges - so this gives you -

Plan D Day 1 Camp at one of the riverside sites near Chames. Day 1 arrive and book in at the site, visit Vallon, stock up with food, buy tickets for both les Bivi, then afternoon paddle down from Vallon to the campsite. Day 2, Pack up camp and pack boats and car then afternoon start on the river to arrive at the first le Bivi campsite, le Gaud before 1800. Day 3 - Start the next morning to arrive at Le Gournier bivi site for lunch. Lazy afternoon exploring. Day 4, early start to beat the rush and arrive down at St Martin for early afternoon. Set up camp at one of the St Martin campsites, Driver buses back with an operator to Pont d'Arc at 1700 to pick up the car whilst rest of team explore Aigueze Camp and supper in St Martin?

Note that if you are short of time, then it is easy to combine the Pont d'Arc stretch with the rest of the Gorges to make a two day trip. This is best out of season when you don't have to worry about planning your trip to dodge the crowds.

Safety

The Gorges de l'Ardèche is a committing trip. It is a minor expedition, where you are at the bottom of a deep gorge and the road is far away so it's reassuring to be well equipped. The Ardèche is notorious for its floods, extremely rare, but especially prevalent in late summer - see page 15, so take notice of any warnings.

La Dent Noire is probably the rapid that causes most damage to people and boats, *la Toupine* is potentially the most dangerous. However, even on an otherwise easy rapid, one of the most dangerous scenarios is being pinned on a rock and other canoes crashing down on top of you - in most capsizes and pins it is best to **immediately exit and swim away from your canoe**. Salvage the boat a few minutes later from the shore when the incident has stabilised and you have had time to assess the situation.

The Ardèche is a busy river and you will probably see quite a few capsizes and minor incidents. Obviously you will help a person in distress, and this is great for international relations, but be careful not to get carried away with your enthusiasm and put your person at risk merely to rescue plastic and metal! (The hire companies normally have guides riding sweep who are expert at salvaging canoes).

Description

Setting off from Chames you immediately have a straight forward bouncy rapid that takes you round the corner. The road now leaves the gorge and there are just high cliffs looming up ahead as you paddle round the circular neck of land that is called *'Pas de Mousse'* At the end of this bend is the first big rapid, **'les Trois Eaux'**, which can often be run down the right hand side of the river - a safe and straight forward line. In low levels, the right channel is often too low and you are then forced to shoot the left hand channel (or portage), which has a drop and a wave at the top, and then often the tail of the rapid sweeps you into the cliff on the left. This can be both an entertaining and photogenic rapid!

Two easier rapids come in the next 2km and help re-establish confidence as the Gorge deepens, the cliffs loom ever closer, the river roars, black clouds threaten from a scowling heaven, the peals of thunder echo off the cliffs - and the dreaded 'Black tooth' rapid looms ahead. Well I have seen it like this! but normally of course the sun is shining, you're having a wonderful time and it is all too easy not to give the infamous **'la Dent Noir'** rapid the respect it deserves.

At this rapid, the river takes a right hand bend and runs against some black cliffs on the left, with a stoney beach on the right. The problem is several black rocks in the middle of the current and there are usually the remains of several plastic canoes wrapped around each one. We strongly recommend that you stop on the beach above on the right to inspect this, and if you have any doubts then wade or line your boat down the top of the rapid. There have been several serious incidents here so in the season, les Pompiers have a safety team on duty (there's a team of about 30 firemen specially trained in river rescue who cover the main rapids in the summer months).

Pont d'Arc

The Pont d'Arc has been a tourist site and one of the natural wonders of Europe for centuries. The river used to take make a huge bend here, flowing where the road now runs - millions of years ago the waters eroded the neck of land and cut through the caves in the limestone to form the arch. The arch is still riddled with caves - one cave runs through the arch on the river right side, linking the upstream and downstream sides, and another pops out near the top of the arch.

In bygones centuries it formed a natural rock bridge for local people, enabling them to cross the river even in times of flood and in 1621 an army of 1200 soldiers struggled across it. The route to the top is a dangerous scramble which used to be popular (the river right side was regarded as the safest), however after several fatal falls officialdom now discourages people from climbing the arch and we are told that the route over the top has been declared illegal under a local ordinance.

The river and gorge now curves round to the left and there are some bubbling little rapids in the next 1.5km which brings you down to **'le Gaud'** bivi site. This used to be an old farm and chateau but is now one of the two official public overnight campsites in the Gorges This is also an emergency first aid, and evacuation post.

You are now in the heart of the Gorges, and continueing on from le Gaud, you can see the great sweep of high cliffs ahead that is the *'Cirque de Gaud'*. At the top of the cliffs, some 270m above the river, is a viewpoint on the 'Route Touristique'. One kilometre down river, the river bends right again with a technical little *rapid 'la Canelle'*, and a big beach on the right. Just though the trees on the right is the old **Chataigneraie** campsite, now owned by PGL, it is no longer a campsite but there is a friendly and welcoming bar that sells **ice cream!** From the beach take a look up at the cliffs opposite and if you are lucky you may see one of the wild goats that often frequent the caves and ledges high above the river. If you need it, there is also a path from here out to the top of the gorge, which brings you out at the road head and a parking place 1km from le Mas de Serret campsite. At the bottom of the beach is another technical rapid *'la Figueras'* which can be quite tricky at some water levels.

Two kilometres, 3 bends, 4 rapids and more magnificent scenery brings you to a sharp left hand bend with cliffs on the right. At the end of these cliffs and about 500m from the bend, is a pebble beach on the right and a steep path that goes up from here to **le Mas de Serret** campsite in approx. 35 minutes.

'la Toupine' rapid - note the current flowing into the cliffs on the left. *Images Actions*

300m below here is one of the longest rapids on the river, **'Gue de Getard'** which gives over 100m of bouncy waves. You can land on the beach above on the left if you want to inspect - this is a great fun run, but beware, it can be a long, rough swim - Fluffy didn't swim, but got very wet on this rapid and wasn't happy. At the bottom of the rapid there are some rock ledges and a stone beach on the right. Another path goes up from here to the PGL centre and campsite at Le Mas de Serret, in about 40 minutes (make sure you keep right when the path forks after 5 minutes.)

Just downstream around the left hand bend is **'le Gournier'** bivouac campsite - pull up on the beach here if you are staying overnight. There is a first aid and evacuation post here. Below the beach is **'la Toupine'** rapid at the start of a 200m section *'le Canal'* where the river has carved a narrow box canyon, with strangely sculptured low limestone cliffs rising straight out of the river. The river is very deep here, with powerful currents and underwater caves. The rapid doesn't look much but sometimes flows straight into the undercut cliffs on the left and so we recommend that you land on the beach above to make a quick inspection - it is normally an easy rapid to run, but potentially a very dangerous place to take a swim.

There is nothing to worry about in 'le Canal' itself, but at the end look out for **'le Grand Gaur'** rapid where the current sweeps you into the rock face on the left. This is shortly followed by *'les Elephants'* - a giant bouncy ride and only a rare risk of trampling. 2km brings you into a long straight section with the high rocks outcrop of *'la Cathedrale'* on the left ahead. There is often a French tricolour flying at the top.

This is the marker for **'la Pastière'** rapid some 300m downstream. This is quite a long rapid with a huge undercut rock in the middle of the current at the bottom with that special property that limestone has for attracting and retaining plastic - in this case very retentive, so this is another rapid we suggest you might want to inspect. In low water it is normally better to head left of the rock.

300m downstream is the private beach and official naturist campsite *'des Templiers'*. The name refers to the Knight of the Templars who in medieval times established a leper colony on the hill opposite. This hill is in a big bend of the river, almost an island, and the food was lowered to the lepers in baskets by ropes from the cliffs above. If you continue around this big bend of the *Cirque de la Madelaine* you can land on a beach to explore the ruins of the lepers houses. There are 3 rapids as you go round this big bend and then another couple of easy rapids in the next km as the river bends left and then right.

At the next sharp bend to the right you will see what looks like a ruined fortress *'les Ramparts du Garn'* on the skyline, but this is in fact just eroded rocks. Immediately below, on the bend is another more difficult rapid called **'le Russe'** with cliffs and rocks on the right, and a beach left. Keep left and close to the beach.

Two rapids and a kilometre past here, around the bend brings you to **'la Cadière'** (affectionately known as *'Knackers Yard'* by the Brits). This is quite a tricky rapid with a good risk of pinning so it's best to land on the beach on the right above to inspect. The river then runs straight and fairly flat for a km and brings you to *'Windy Corner'* with a huge overhanging cliff on the right as the river takes a sharp turn to the left. There's a couple of easy rapids in the next km as you approach the last big bend. The small campsite on the left is *'les Grottes'* and then the cliffs start to drop away, and the gorge starts to widen as you go around the bend. There's lots of people, sun bathing and swimming from the rock ledges that border the river and you get your first sight of the road, just 80m above, with tourists looking out from the viewpoint and waving. Rest awhile here if you have the time and take your last chance for a swim in the Gorges.

Two km brings you to **Sauze** and you are jolted back into the world of traffic and tourism - with huge fleets of mini buses and trailers lined up here waiting to collect the hire canoes. You can take out here or keep right, shoot the easy rapid and take out almost anywhere in the next km down to St Martin.

You will see the ramparts and building of **Aiguèze** up on top of the cliffs on your right, and if you have time to spare, we recommend landing at the old ferry site below and climbing up the path to explore this beautifully restored medieval village - don't worry there's also a café and ice creams there, in a much pleasanter, cooler ambience than St Martin.

The long suspension bridge at St Martin is one of the classics that you see in all those old Second World War films - it's narrow approach now terrorises English coach drivers. Immediately below the bridge is a wide stone weir with a glissière, then some 300m below is a beach and *'le Moulin'* campsite on the left. You can continue, if wanted some 11km to the confluence with the Rhone and the ancient town of Pont St Esprit, but the river is flat, wide, shallow and pretty boring, and after the magnificence of the Gorges de l'Ardèche - who would want to? You now have a classic, famous river under your belt and are all set now to explore the less popular but equally good rivers in the rest of this guide....Good Paddling!

Dipper

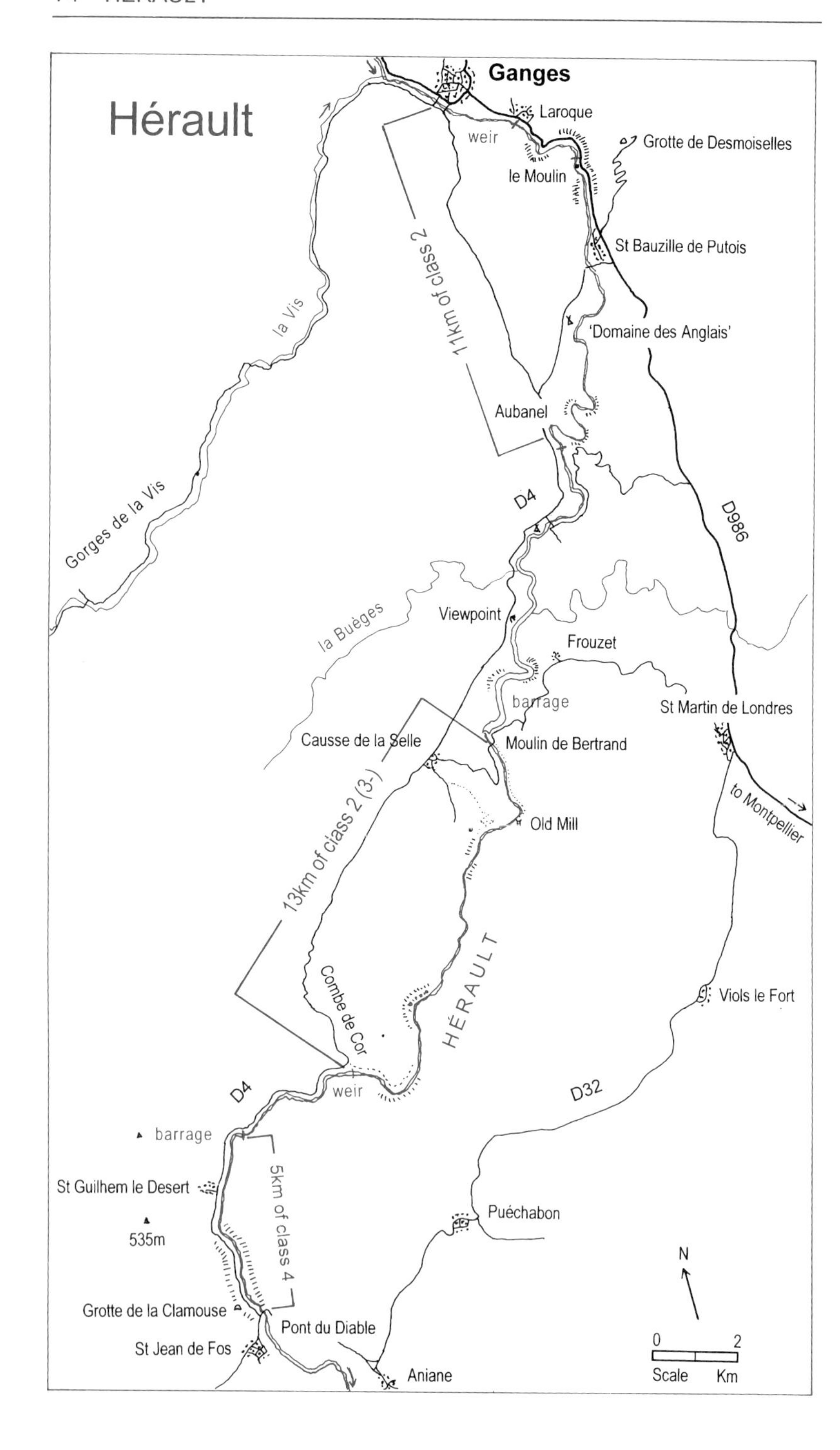

Hérault
Ganges
Laroque
weir
Grotte de Desmoiselles
le Moulin
St Bauzille de Putois
11km of class 2
la Vis
'Domaine des Anglais'
Aubanel
Gorges de la Vis
D4
D986
la Buèges
Viewpoint
Frouzet
barrage
St Martin de Londres
Causse de la Selle
Moulin de Bertrand
to Montpellier
Old Mill
13km of class 2 (3-)
HÉRAULT
Combe de Cor
Viols le Fort
D4
weir
D32
barrage
5km of class 4
St Guilhem le Desert
Puéchabon
535m
N
Grotte de la Clamouse
Pont du Diable
St Jean de Fos
0
2
Scale
Km
Aniane

Hérault

Summary

Ganges to Aubanel	2 (3-)	13	★★	✤✤	☺☺	<200	small river, diverse scenic run.
Moulin de Bertrand >	2	11	★	✤✤	☺	<50	a wild green canyon.
St Guilhem to Pont d.d	4	5	★★	✤✤	-	<10	convoluted run for deviant kayakers

A highly picturesque gorge only 40 km from the Mediterranean coast and offering three very different sections for paddling.

The River

A coastal plain just 20km wide separates the Massif Central from the Mediterranean and over the centuries this has echoed to the march of conquering armies and marauding bands - the Phoenicians bands, Roman Legion, Gothic hordes, and Saracen armies, all swept along this natural corridor and fertile plain. To escape them, the locals headed for the hills, via a narrow, forbidding gorge from where narrow paths led to hidden caves and villages. This is the historic gorge of the Hérault.

Compared to its more famous sister rivers of the Tarn and the Ardèche it's a river that has stayed little known outside French paddling circles. A quality river with some great scenery and few paddlers, this river is definitely worth a visit! The river rises some 30km north of Ganges on the slopes of Mont Aigual 1567m and not far from the Gorges du Tarn. In summer months it can be paddled from Ganges and this first section was Fluffy's favourite - perhaps the most scenic and lots of fun. Two hydro dams and horrid sterile reservoirs follow, and then there is a wild green canyon section leading down to the famous village of St Guilem le Desert. Below here is the last section which is more difficult and is of main appeal to deviant white water kayakers - the river cuts through the last of the plateau in a narrow convoluted gorge with fantastic rock formations and strange shoots and drops. The river disgorges onto the coastal plain at the Pont du Diable, an old 'Roman' bridge and beauty spot. From here to the coast it is flat and uninspiring with many weirs.

Canoe Camping

Not recommended - the different paddling sections are separated by huge hydro dams and associated reservoirs. It's worth noting that wild camping in this region is strongly discouraged because of the risks of forest fire - the area is densely forested and high winds are prevalent in the summer months.

Off the river

St Guilhem le Désert is one of the best preserved and most beautiful mediaeval villages in Europe and as such has been declared a UNESCO World Heritage Site. Obviously a 'must do' is to have a wander round, but we suggest that this is best done in the early evening when most of the day tourists have headed home. For the energetic there are several hill walks to viewpoints some 400m above the village.

The *Grotte des Desmoiselles* (www.desmoiselles.com) near Ganges is one of the great show caverns of France and a major tourist site, and the *Grotte de Clamouse* is another tourist show cave (www.clamouse.com). About one hour's drive west of Ganges is another prime tourist sight, the *'Cirque de Navacelles'*.

In terms of outdoor activities this area is perhaps a little more limited than some (or perhaps we didn't spend enough time on the right kind of research) but canyoning, via ferata, and mountain biking are available - ask at the Ganges tourist office for more information. The beaches, water sports, and night clubs of the Mediterranean are only about an hour's drive away so if you've never swam in the Med, then this is your chance. A closer alternative to the Med, is the beach *at Pont du Diable* where we recommend the cheap and friendly snack bar/restaurant. You can drive down over the old bridge to the snack bar and then spend a sunny afternoon swimming, and paddling up into the gorge for lazing, playing, jumping and diving off the cliffs.

Food and drink

Ganges has a good selection of restaurants, and so does the more touristy St Guilhem - try the *'Petit Jardin'* here. Local paddlers recommend *'le Bougainvillier'*, a typical French restaurant that serves good food, around 12 Euros for dinner, 500m from the bridge at Saint Beauzille de Putois; also *'la Bergerie du Bayle'* at Frouzet, 3km east of the Moulin de Bertrand.

Camping

There are several riverside campsites on the top half of the river, but none on the second stretch or near St Guilhem. On the top stretch, *'Camping du Domaine d'Anglas'* (Tel: 04 67 73 70 18) struck us as one of the pleasantest riverside sites and with good facilities. At Ganges, *'Tivoli Camping'* (tel: 04 67 57 92 97) could be used to put in and is convenient for the town. If you want to camp nearer the Mediterranean then *'le Moulin de Siau'* is a pleasant shady site just outside Aniane (tel: 04 67 57 51 08)

Maps and Guides

IGN Top25 sheet 2742ET covers the top stretch and sheet 2642ET covers the bottom sections around St Guilhem. A good buy is the IGN Top 100 sheet 65 which covers both the Hérault and the Orb.

Tourist Offices - www.stguilhem.com

Ganges, tel: 04 67 73 00 56, fax: 04 67 73 00 50.
St Guilhem, tel: 04 67 57 44 33.

Canoe Hire and rafting

Canoe de Moulin, tel: 04 67 73 30 73 www.canoe-france.com
Antalya, tel: 04 67 73 11 11 www.canoe34.com
Kayapuna, tel: 04 67 57 30 25
Canoes de St Guilhem, tel: 04 67 57 44 99
Canoe la Vallee des Moulins, tel: 04 67 73 12 45
Canoe Rapido, tel: 04 67 55 75 75

Other rivers

The Vis flows into the Hérault just upstream of Ganges and in good water levels - normally spring or Autumn, the upper section from the famous Cirque de Navacelles is supposed to be a 3 star paddle at class 3(4). In higher flows the upper Hérault can also be paddled from Gasquet, class 3(4). The Orb is about 2 hours drive away.

Ganges to Aubanel	**13 km of class 2 (3-)**	★★	❉❉	☺☺
Water quality - OK.	Temp. - warm. 5 cumecs?		Busy? <200	

Summary

A small river running through a highly scenic gorge and with some fun rapids - mainly bedrock. Our group all enjoyed this and rated it as better than the Chasezac and les Defiles d'Ardeche. For the top part of this run the road is close to the river so a good idea of the rapids can be got as you drive up the valley.

In summer months there is usually insufficient water above Ganges, however, although the flow is small we only had to wade and push off a couple of times and then only when we got the line wrong.

Description

Put in at Ganges on the left bank on some public park land below the old bridge and close to the Gendarmerie, or alternatively at the campsite. A few stony, shallow rapids flowing under trees brings you down to the picturesque village of **Laroque** with a mediaeval tower and church overlooking the river. There is a sloping weir here, about 2m high that should be either portaged on the right, or in low water it may be possible to land on the weir and slide it over.

Hérault - a peaceful stretch below Moulin de Bertrand.

Just under a km and a small rapid or two brings you to **le 'Grand S'**, which is a steep rocky shoot going right of an island on a right hand bend. This seems to have been designed such that hire boats just bounce over the rocks, whereas private canoes get swamped and trashed! Definitely a class 2, maybe a 3- and you might want to scout this before running it. This is followed by **le 'Petit S'** which is just around the left hand bend that follows - more fun and waves capable of swamping an open canoe.

Settle back now, and take your time over the next, most scenic section of the river - for the next km the river takes a long bend around to the right and has carved a 200m deep gorge through the surrounding hills. The gorge is U shaped in cross section with rock ledges sloping gently up out of the river, then curving up and steepening to become cliffs fringing the skyline. All white limestone and very picturesque and impressive, and made more so by the buzzards soaring over the cliffs - only slightly marred by the road close by. No more than a gentle current, but deep water, so this is a great spot for a swim, a picnic and perhaps some seal launches?

La 'Rapide des Piquets' is fairly obvious with its line of old piles along the top of an old weir - this just needs a careful approach so that you get the right line. About 200m below you can see the old Mill which is now a canoe base. A long class 2 rapid leads down past the mill and gives you an opportunity to pose (or make an idiot of yourself) in front of the canoe hire customers.

The river now flows out of the gorge and the village of **St Bauzille de Putois** is on the left. The suspension bridge comes into sight and about 200m above it is a short rocky drop on the right. There is a public beach, with parking on the left at this bridge which is called the *'Pont due Fer'* by locals.

After the bridge, the river widens and mellows out, becoming mainly flat with grade 1 rapids over gravel bars. Both banks are densely lined with overhanging trees and the view is just a green river and green trees. However, a canoe base comes up after a km and offers ice creams to relieve the boredom. Another km brings you to the *'Domaine Anglaise'* campsite which is just before a sharp bend to the right.

The river now changes character yet again as it bends, twists and cuts through a series of rocky ridges. This feels a wild section with cliffs on each bend, rocky ledges making easy bedrock rapids, no buildings, no road, few people, and just a scrubby hillside in sight.

Four kilometre after the campsite and a field and building is visible on the right on a left hand bend. This is the **take out** - it is only 400m to the dangerous **'Barrage de Vernede'** and this section is 'interdit'. The field at the take out is leased by a rafting company who may require payment if you wish to park here.

Below the dam is the *Restaurant du Barrage* and the *'Val d'Hérault'* campsite is in the next 3km of river before the start of the 6km long reservoir.

Moulin de Bertrand to Combe de Cor		**11 km of class 2**	★	❁❁	☺
Water quality - OK.	Temp. - warm	7 cumecs?		Busy? <50	

Summary

A steep sided, wild, wooded canyon, 200m deep, with no buildings and few signs of civilisation. Numerous class 1 and 2 rapids maintain interest for most of the run.

Description

Put in immediately upstream of the bridge at the **Moulin de Bertrand** down some steep steps on the right bank. There is limited parking and private canoeists are not welcomed by the canoe hire company based here - they wouldn't even let Fluffy buy an ice cream!

Looking back upstream you can see the dramatic high dam, downstream heavily forested valley sides slope up steeply to the skyline. Once you leave the bridge behind there are no roads, paths, buildings, or other sign of human activity except for an occasional canoe. The river starts easy with straight-forward class 1 stoney rapids.

After 2km the river bends to the right and there is a well preserved ancient mill on the left, the **'Moulin de Figueres'** which is well worth stopping to explore. In another setting this would have been carefully restored and be a prime tourist sight, but in this remote location, all overgrown and wild, it is more impressive and fascinating. You can crawl through the mill tunnels, admire the solid building plan that has enabled the mill to survive the floods of centuries, see the original mill wheels, and look up at the fortified room above where the miller must have lived with his family.

Paddling off down the river again, note the ruined tower high up on the skyline on the right bank. The rapids are all class one, however, just as you are getting a bit bored the river bends, some cliffs appear either side, and there's a fine bouncy class 2 rapid on the bend. The river then intersperses class 1-2 rapids with occasional flat stretches and chance to look around - kingfishers darting out from the trees, a host of brightly coloured butterflies, and a few eagles soaring high over the cliffs.

A long bend to left marks *'les cent fonts'* - a long line of springs just above the river level on the right. Then after 2 km the river bends slowly right again and becomes flat. A strange stone beehive building on the left marks an old water intake and another km brings you to the dam and suggested **take out** - on the right up to the road, where there is plenty of parking. If you prefer to continue then portage the dam on the left, taking care to avoid the water intake and its associated sign 'Danger d'aspiration'! There is another 3km down to the next dam, but it doesn't have a great deal to recommend it - the lower part of this is reservoir and may be dry in the summer, with the water flowing out of the bottom of the dam through a dangerous tunnel.

St Guilhem to Pont du Diable **5 km of class 4** ★★ ❀❀ -

Water quality - OK. Temperature - warm Busy? <10

Summary

At extremely low summer levels (5 cumecs? when we were there) this is a highly picturesque, narrow, rock gorge, mainly flat but with six class 3 drops - and with kayaks, all easily scouted and portaged if wanted. However, at more normal summer levels and higher flows the river becomes much more difficult and dangerous - so inspect this section very carefully (and the reservoir upstream) before doing it. This is why we have given it a class 4 rating.

British paddlers might compare this stretch to parts of the Welsh upper Conwy or the Scottish Spean Gorge. The drops are fairly obvious and mostly visible from the road. The rock is limestone, sculptured by the water into strange convoluted shapes. Half way down the run is a beautiful box canyon where springs waterfall through a green mossy curtain of vegetation on the left bank.

. With river flows 8 or 10 cumecs most of the rapids are class 4, some are really dangerous, (2 big stoppers at the beginning and one syphon at the end!) and the portages are also then really difficult. Note that the barrage can release between 5 to18 cumecs at any time, however this is only likely to happen when there is some water in the reservoir. Be prepared for the water level to increase at any time.

Description

It is probably best to start this run just downstream of the dam where there is a small bridge over a stream from the right. From this point, the river starts quietly, there is only one class 3 rapid before Saint Guilhem, however you will find a few play spots for a warm up before arriving at the "Combe de Brunan" where there is a 2m drop and an old mill. This is the start of the gorge proper and its six or so tight drops.

Take note of the last drop, 200m above the bridge, where the current syphons under some huge blocks. This is potentially dangerous and should be scouted and either portaged right or perhaps run left - class 5? From here it is flat as you paddle under the old Pont du Diable to take out at the beach below.

The whole canyon is highly photogenic so Fluffy and companion used the well worn camera ploy - "you should really have someone taking photos" - to get out of doing this run.

Mallard

Hérault - shooting a drop in the gorge above le Pont du Diable.

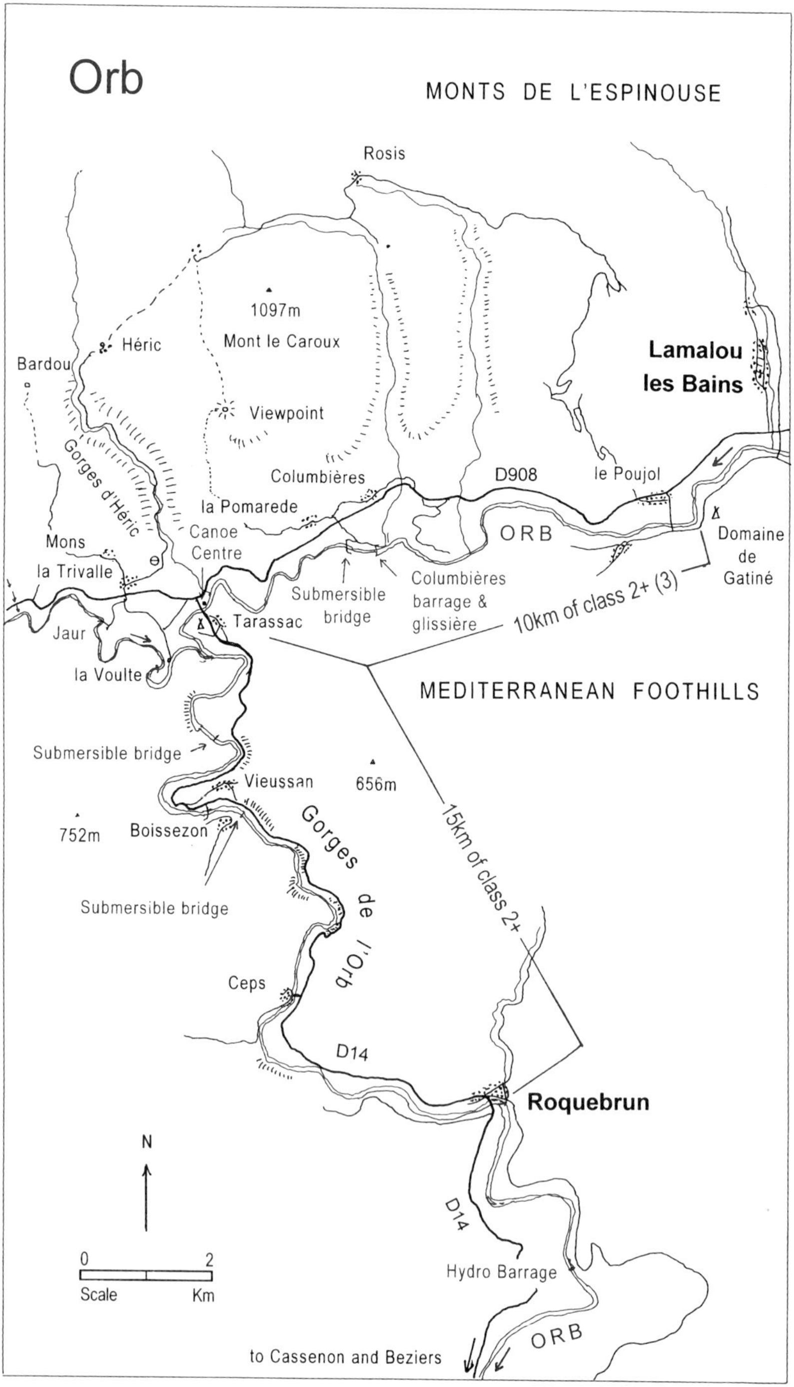

Orb

MONTS DE L'ESPINOUSE

Rosis

1097m

Mont le Caroux

Héric

Bardou

Viewpoint

Lamalou les Bains

Gorges d'Héric

Columbières

D908

le Poujol

la Pomarede

Mons

Canoe Centre

ORB

Domaine de Gatiné

la Trivalle

Submersible bridge

Columbières barrage & glissière

10km of class 2+ (3)

Jaur

Tarassac

la Voulte

MEDITERRANEAN FOOTHILLS

Submersible bridge

Vieussan

656m

752m

Boissezon

Gorges de l'Orb

15km of class 2+

Submersible bridge

Ceps

D14

Roquebrun

N

0 2

Scale Km

D14

Hydro Barrage

ORB

to Cassenon and Beziers

Orb

Summary

Poujol to Tarassac	2+	10	★★★	❁❁	-	<50	Fine rapids and a wild valley.
Tarasac to Roquebrun	2(2+)	15	★★★	❁❁❁	☺	<200	'Gorges de l'Orb' - superb canoeing.

The River

At first we were disbelieving when friends told us about this river - "really good class 2-3, only 30 km from the Med, good water levels in the summer, and hardly anyone on it". We thought "they've got to be joking, but we'd better go and check it out" - so duly did and everything was just how they said, a really fine classic river ideal for open canoes and with good water levels in the middle of August.

The scenery is grand rather than spectacular, with mighty vistas of a clear green river and rolling green forested hill sides. This reminded us of some fine Scottish river, but of course its not Scotland - its hot and sunny, the water is warm, and there are no midges. There's lots of other insect, bird and fish life though and this is a great river for nature-loving adults (Charlotte, William and Thomas thought the upper Herault was more fun though). At the beginning of June the area is full of cherry trees, with lots growing wild by the roadside.

The secret to its good white water are two huge reservoirs in the mountains to the north, which normally release sufficient water to guarantee decent water levels even in the height of summer. The Orb is the most southern river in this guidebook and in terms of the paddling, one of the best!

Canoe Camping

Perhaps not an obvious first choice as a multi-day trip, on reflection it would probably make an excellent white water touring trip in open canoes and it could be made into a leisurely 3 day trip by continuing on another 10 km to Cessenon.

Off the river

We were fascinated, and would have liked to have spent more time in this interesting area which seems to have been largely by-passed by tourism - just sleepy historic villages nestling in deep valleys amongst the wooded limestone hills. Only recently has the natural beauty of the region been recognised and the area designated the 'Parc Naturel Regional du Haut Languedoc'. The *Monts de l'Espinouse* tower 1000m immediately to the north of the Orb and on a clear day offer offer stunning views south to the Mediterranean and across to the Pyrénéés. Feisty fell runners will want to tackle this from the valley bottom, wimps however you can take the car up to Douch at 897m and then there is an easy 2km walk to the table d'orientation at 1039m which overlooks the Orb valley. Colombières is popular for rock climbing, with a huge swimming pool for partying in afterwards.

Cleaved through these mountains is the *Gorges d'Héric*, a narrow, spectacular and pretty canyon just 2 km from *Tarassac* - a great evening's walk or bike ride, and a popular place for rock climbing and picnics next to the clear sparkling stream with some great swimming pools and water slides. A narrow tarmac road runs up the valley, prohibited to all motorised vehicles, except a little tourist tractor train that runs when there is sufficient demand. At the top is the picturesque mountain hamlet of Héric. On the Jaur, Olargues with its old medieval bridge is well worth a visit.

For the lovers of sand and sun, the small beach resort of Valras Plage on the Med is less than an hour's drive, whilst for the garden lover we recommend a stroll around the famous *'Jardin Méditerranean'* in the picturesque village of *Roquebrun.*

The local tourist offices can advise on other hiking and mountain bike trips, also canyoning, rock climbing, and bungy jumping.

Food and drink

There's a cheap and cheerful restaurant on the campsite at Tarassac, or for more choice you are better driving up the valley to **Lamalou les Bains** which is an old Spa town and has several excellent and cheap restaurants.

Camping

There are river side campsites at Poujol, Tarassac, Roquebrun and Cassenon.

The municipal campsite at **Tarassac** is a 2 star site with a bathing beach, and popular with generations of French family campers. It's well shaded and cheap, but it is a large busy site so booking ahead is a good idea - tel: 046797 72 64 We found that it wasn't too noisy, but if you are looking for a quieter and more spacious site then you are probably better off at the newer private campsite *'Domaine de Gatiné'* at the put in at **le Poujol** which has a small swimming pool, and grass terraces.

If you arrive late at night and just need somewhere to park up, then the *'Air de l'Albine'* is a deserted picnic site just downstream of the barrage at Colombieres.

Maps and Guides

A new IGN Top25 sheet is planned as we go to press that should cover the area Olargues-Lamalou-Roquebrun. Slightly less detailed but good for walking, is the 1:10,000 map of Mount Caroux. IGN Top 100 sheet 65 covers both the Hérault and the Orb at a scale of 1:100,000, so is a best buy if you are paddling both rivers.

Tourist Offices - www.herault-en-languedoc.com

Lamalou les Bains, tel: 04 67 95 64 17
Mons la Trivalle, tel: 04 67 97 71 70
Roquebrun, tel: 04 67 89 79 97

Canoe Hire and rafting

Tarassac, Atelier Riviere Randonnee, (Ecole FFCK), tel: 04 67 97 74 64.
Roquebrun, Grandeur Nature, tel: 04 67 89 52 90.

Other rivers

The **Jaur** can often be paddled in summer months *from Moulin Napoleon Pisciculture.* This gives about 5 km of class 2-3, if there is sufficient water being released from the hydro station just upstream (the water comes through a tunnel under the mountain from the huge Lac du Lauzas reservoir.) A barrage and small hydro plant at la Voulte normally leaves the big bend dry and requires a short portage across the isthmus.

The **Orb** upstream of Le Poujol normally has insufficient water levels for paddling in the summer months, but earlier in the season can be paddled from *Sérieys*, described as 23 km of class 2(3) with numerous barrages (check with the canoe base at Tarassac Mill for more information).

If you are a play boater, you might want to check out the rapids at **Reals**, 6 km downstream from Cessenon, described as 500m of class 3-4.

Poujol to Tarassac	**10 km of class 2+**	★★★	❀❀	-
Water quality - good	Temp.- warm. 10 cumecs?		Busy?	<50

Summary

This is superb paddle with some well defined technical rapids in a scenic and wild valley. There are only distant views of the road and villages which are high on the valley sides above the river. The impressive 1000m high flanks of Mount Caroux overlook the valley on its north side and to the south are the densely forested foothills of St Michel.

Description

We recommend a **put in** close to the *'Domaine de Gatinee'* campsite on the left bank, upstream of the bridge at **le Poujol sur Orb**. (A start at Lamalou les Bains is also possible and gives an additional 2km of flat water warm up, or if you want a shorter run then the barrage at *Colombières* is an alternative put in).

The suspension bridge just downstream of the campsite is noteworthy for its warning signs. 'No entry if the temperature is -20°C or less' makes one wonder what the winters are like here - packs of wolves roaming up a frozen river? Polar bears foraging from the ice floes of the Med? Let your mind wander as you paddle along and enjoy a river temperature around 17°C and air temperature probably 30°C. The paddling is easy with just a few class 1 rapids over shingle beds and fine views ahead of the *Monts de l'Espinouse* looming up 1000m above the river.

Orb - some intriguing road signs.

After some 3 km the river bends south away from the road and the views become noticeably wilder with densely wooded hills the only thing to see on the south side of the river. The first notable rapid comes after another 500m or so, a big bouldery drop class 2+. Then as you round the long bend the village and church tower of **Colombières** comes into view high on the valley side.

A km of flat water brings you to the remains of a concrete barrage which can usually be run down a concrete shoot on the right - inspect first for any obstructions. This is immediately followed by long, technical class 2+ rapid which finishes in another long flat stretch - time for salvage and rescue perhaps.... This is the lead up to the 3m high **Colombières barrage** - this is fairly obvious with a large square stone building at the right hand end. The barrage can normally be run by an exhilarating glissière down the centre - marked by some green posts. (Note that if driving to here you need to turn off the main road opposite the signed turning to *Pomerède*).

Below the barrage are some 300m of fun class 2 rapid down to a 'submersible' concrete bridge that can be shot in low water levels if you hunker down in your boat - but at higher levels this could be distinctly dodgey!

Now comes the best of the run - some 4 km of classic grade 2 white water as the river twists through green densely wooded valley sides with occasional glimpses of ancient villages high on the slopes of Monts de l'Espinouse. The river is more constrained and whooshes along with a good current and on every bend are low cliffs and a fine little technical rapid - nothing too difficult, but keep an eye out for overhanging trees and sweepers.

As you come round the last bend the main road and some buildings are faintly visible through the trees - keep right and pull in to scout if you wish because the next rapid is slightly harder, class 3-, and leads you down to the slalom site above **Tarassac Mill**. The class 2 rapids of the slalom site follow immediately, with big boulders, clean shoots, and well defined eddies - making this a joy to paddle.

Below these rapids is a stretch of flat water and a bar and café, so a good place to land and scout the next mill rapid over an ice cream. This is a long technical, testing, class 3 rapid (well, testing for me in that I confess I swam on it!) which can be portaged, if wanted, on the left - or you could of course, with permission, take out here. There is 300m of flat below in which to salvage canoes and gear (but I never regained all my pride.) and then an easy but incredibly rocky rapid - all bump and scrape - leads down to the municipal beach and campsite - ice creams and cold beers just 50m up the track!

Tarassac to Roquebrun **15 km of class 2 (2+)** ★★★ ❀❀❀ ☺

Water quality - good. Temp. - warm. 15 cumecs? Busy? <50

Summary

This stretch compares in quality to the one before with over 30 rapids and over half of these class 2. One of our group called it "classic grade 2 - superb for open canoes". The Jaur tributary brings in more water - so the rapids are perhaps a little less technical than the preceding stretch, and a little bit more bouncy! There is a good current and hardly any flat stretches.

The river cuts through the last range of foothills to the Mediterranean plain, in a winding gorge and whilst this stretch is less wild, it's just as scenic with hillsides covered in green woods, orchards, pastures and old terraced vin yards, whilst ancient villages gleam white in the hot Mediterranean sun.

Description

Put in at the Municipal Beach and campsite at **Tarassac**. Two little 'bump and scrape' rapids, perhaps easy class 2, lead down to the confluence with the **Jaur**. After this the fun starts with rapids every 500m or so, many class 2, and some long and rocky; so there's not much time for just drifting, looking down through the clear water and counting the trout.

3 km after the confluence with the Jaur is another **'Submersible' concrete bridge**. In the summer season this will normally be well signed and a portage right is recommended for beginners. Check the bridge out, however, because at normal low flows there is probably about 60cm of headroom and you may decide that it can be safely shot. At higher flows, these submersible bridges can be a real death trap: there may be little or no headroom, or if the river is flowing over the top of the bridge, then the tunnel will form a syphon that may be blocked by debris ... definitely not a nice experience!

Going round the next bend, the old village of *Vieussan* comes into view on the left with an ancient ruined tower dominating the skyline. The river sweeps round the village in a big bend so its over 2km before **Vieussan Bridge** comes in sight with a bouncy class 2+ rocky shoot and rock ledges on the left. This rapid (we counted it as no. 12) usually makes a fine surf wave, playspot, and a good excuse for an early lunch.

500m below Vieussan Bridge is an even more dangerous **'Submersible bridge'** with only some 140 cm of headroom in low water. Land on the right to scout and portage. The good paddling and rapids continue with another class 2+ rapid at the old mill, '*Moulin de Graise*', about a km downstream. This is probably the best part of the **'Gorges de l'Orb'** - the road is now high up out of sight, the valley sides climb steeply over 300m and the river has carved high cliffs on each bend. We found it all very reminiscent of the Ardèche, with the same clear water, great little class 2 rapids, and rock ledges lining the river - all that was missing were the crowds!

This lovely 3km section finishes at the village of **Ceps** where you can land or take out if wanted upstream of the bridge on the left. We were a bit disappointed to find no bars or ice cream shops in this pretty, sleepy little village so Fluffy naturally insisted on continuing down river. The valley and river widen a little but there are still some 12 or so rapids in the 5km down to **Roquebrun** and the paddle is probably worth it just for the view of this highly picturesque village perched on the hillside above the old stone bridge - all white houses, orange clay roofs, and green gardens.

We recommend **taking out** upstream of the bridge on the left bank where there is a convenient quiet, '*Parking Esplanade*'. (Fluffy insisted on first calling in at the canoe base opposite for an ice cream). The next big village of *Cessenon* is 10km downstream, but the river progressively gets wider and flatter, with one barrage and glissière after 5km.

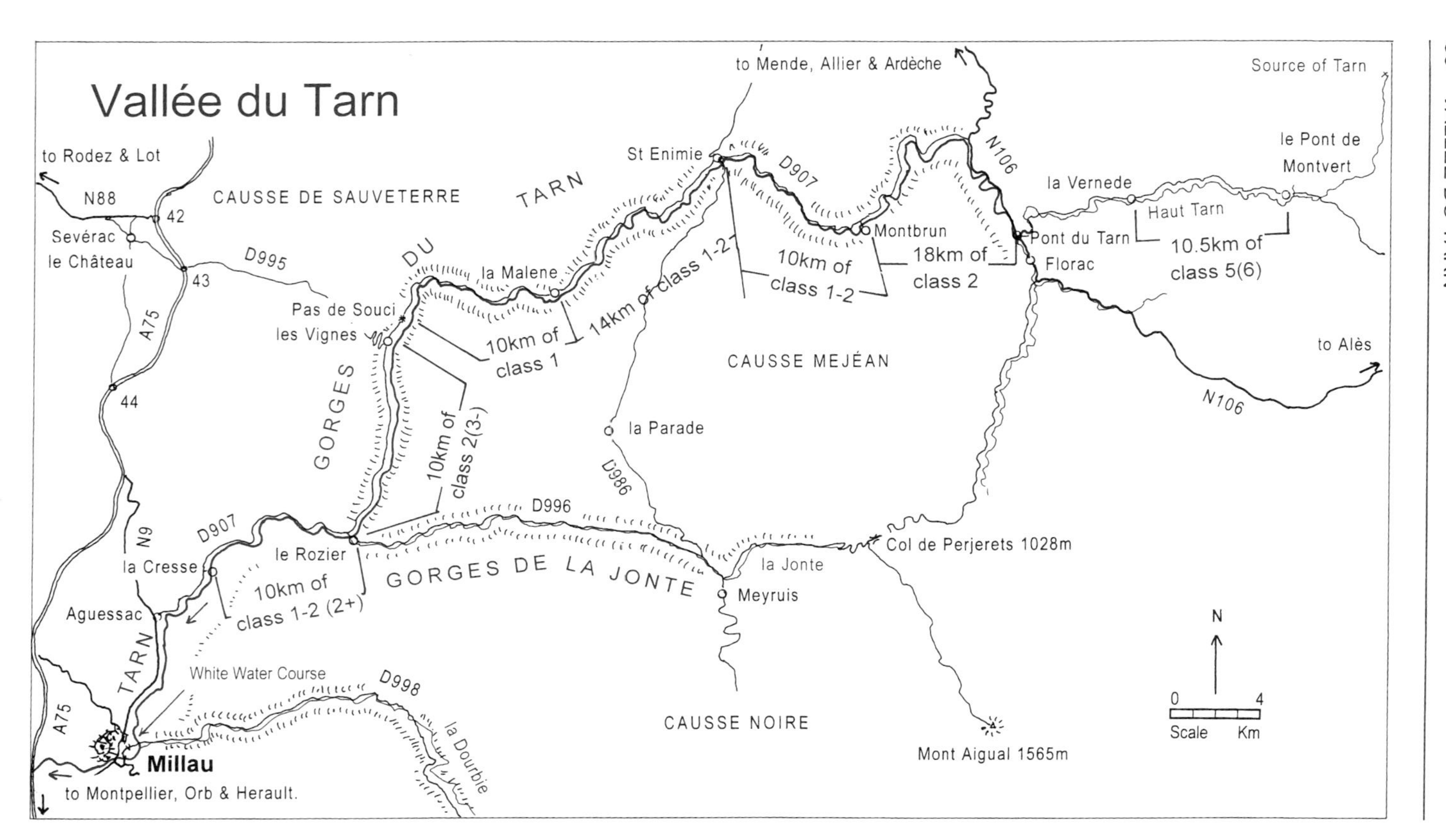

Vallée du Tarn
to Rodez & Lot
N88
42
CAUSSE DE SAUVETERRE
TARN
Sevérac
le Château
43
D995
DU
la Malene
St Enimie
to Mende, Allier & Ardèche
D907
N106
Montbrun
la Vernede
Haut Tarn
le Pont de
Montvert
Source of Tarn
Pont du Tarn
Florac
10.5km of
class 5(6)
18km of
class 2
10km of
class 1-2
14km of class 1-2
10km of
class 1
Pas de Souci
les Vignes
A75
44
GORGES
CAUSSE MEJÉAN
to Alès
N106
la Parade
10km of
class 2(3-)
D986
D996
N9
D907
le Rozier
Col de Perjerets 1028m
la Cresse
la Jonte
10km of
class 1-2 (2+)
GORGES DE LA JONTE
Meyruis
Aguessac
TARN
N
White Water Course
D998
0 4
Scale Km
A75
CAUSSE NOIRE
la Dourbie
Millau
Mont Aigual 1565m
to Montpellier, Orb & Herault.

Tarn

Summary

River and run	Class	Km	Stars	Scen.	Fluffy	Busy	Notes
le Pont du Tarn >	2-3	18	★★	❁❁	-	<10	*Usually insufficient water in Jul-Aug.*
Montbrun >	1-2	10	★	❁❁	☺☺	<50	Scenic introduction
Sainte Enimie >	1-2	14	★★	❁❁❁	☺☺	<200	Old villages & deep gorges
La Malene to Ps de sc	1	10	★★★	❁❁❁	☺☺	>200	Spectacular and popular run.
les Vignes to le Rozier	2 (3-)	10	★★★	❁❁❁	☺	<200	Wild water and wilder scenery
le Rozier to la Cresse	1-2 (2+)	10	★	❁❁	☺	<200	Valley now wider.

A spectacular deep canyon, long lines of high limestone cliffs glowing in the sunset, a crystal clear turquoise river, white rocks and small beaches, green wooded valley sides, griffin vultures soaring high overhead, ancient villages slumbering under the hot Mediterranean sun - these are the famous 'Gorges du Tarn'

The River

These are some of the most impressive limestone canyons of the Massif Central, where the river has cut a 500m deep cleft through the plateau of the Causses and the plateau and gorges are now protected as the "Parc Regional des Grandes Causses". Famous as a tourist site and a beauty spot, in high summer it is busy, but not unbearably so - I first paddled these gorges with the famous Everest paddler Dr Mike Jones in 1975 - 25 years later, even in high summer the gorges retain their charm and we were pleasantly surprised at how much we enjoyed the gorges and the paddling. The cliffs and gorges were impressive as I remembered them, but I had forgotten just how forested and wild the valley sides appear and was thrilled to see several eagles and griffin vultures circling high over the cliffs.

Even in the driest August you will always find enough water to paddle, this is probably because much of the water flow appears to come from 'resurgents' - springs and underground streams flowing into the river as the gorges cut their way through the water table lying under the limestone plateau. The water is crystal clear, so that you can clearly see the round white stones on the bottom of the river and the huge trout (that are a speciality of the local restaurants).

Only 90km over the watershed from the Ardèche gorges, the river and cliffs are somewhat comparable - the Tarn is a deeper canyon but not as remote as it has a road running up the valley - out of sight for most of the time and the road does make for easy shuttles.

The Tarn is easily accessed by the A75 autoroute. We recommend taking exit 42 and approaching the Gorges via the Point Sublime so that your first sight is a magnificent view from the top of the escarpment.

Canoe Camping

The Tarn is a classic river for canoe camping, normally run as a 4 or 5 day trip from Montbrun down to Millau. There is a good diversity of both paddling and scenery, plenty of campsites, and a good road up the valley for the return. The only problem is the 1km portage along the road needed at the Pas de Souci (see description in following section) - perhaps a taxi?

Off the river

The valley is famous for its ancient villages and churches that are great places for an evening stroll. Many of them are floodlit on summer nights. Sainte Enimie is the historic medieval centre of the valley, with old houses, cobbled streets and a 12th century church and abbey. Also an excellent tourist information centre.

There are some great **hikes** here up to viewpoints overlooking the gorges - 'up' being the key word, as the top of the cliffs are 500m above the river! Note that the 'sentier de la vallee du Tarn' follows the left hand bank of the river for the whole length of the gorge (with quite a bit of ups and downs) so offers an activity option for the non-paddler.

Mountain biking is a bit limited here because of the deep and narrow gorge but the main road up the valley is relatively quiet in the evening time - we used it then for some pleasant cycle shuttles. The tracks indicated as dashed lines on our map can normally be cycled. If you are looking for longer bike rides, then there is plenty of scope up on the plateau of the Causse exploring its ancient villages and culture - the tour du Causse Méjan is a long route that follows old paths along the edge of the plateau.

We recommend the 'Maison du Parc' and the ecology museum at Florac if you would like to know more about the ancient culture of the Causses.

The magnificent cliffs of dolomitic limestone obviously make this into something of a Mecca for **climbers** with le Rozier as one of the main centres. There are also some fine cave systems to explore, mainly centred on Meyruis to the East. Local operators offer **canyoning** and potholing. On the riverside downstream of les Vignes is a fine high ropes course, open to all. Other popular family attractions are a wild animal park and a vulture centre.

Ask the local tourist office for information leaflets on any of these activities.

Food and drink

The nice thing about being in a tourist area is that there is always plenty of ice cream shops, bars and restaurants! - and plenty of choice in all the main villages. Outside of the more usual restaurants we recommend the small pizzaria at **Castelbouc** set in sylvan surroundings, overlooking the river and with a traditional wood fired oven.

On the other side of the river at **Prades**, on the main road in the village and run by an old couple, is one of those simple, traditional French restaurants that are a delight to discover: totally untouristy, just a small room and spartan furniture, simple but good cooking, no fancy menu, only two choices of main dish, but 4 courses, and wine for 12 euros complete! Further down the valley, the *Hotel le Parisian* at **Les Vignes** is more up market, but offers good food and value.

Camping

There is a wide choice of campsites of all standards but the more popular ones may be fully booked in high season. We found a beautiful pastoral 2 star site on the banks of the river just downstream from **Prades** - trees, grass, cliffs and the river - rather basic facilities but great value. The campsites at **Le Rosier** were a bit too busy for our liking, but we found the riverside site at **Les Vignes** *'les Teroires'* to be clean, pleasant, and very convenient. Other canoeists with young families have recommended the site at **Peyreleau** and *'les Fayards'* site downstream of **St Enimie**, which has two fine beaches.

Maps and Guides

IGN Top25 sheet 2649 OT "Gorges du Tarn" covers the whole of the gorges at a scale of 1:25,000 and is well worth buying if you are going to spend some time here. IGN Top 100 sheet 58 covers a wider area of the Tarn valley and also the upper and middle Lot at a scale of 1:100,000 so is another good buy.

Tourist Offices - www.gorgesdutarn.com

St Enimie Tel: 04 66 48 53 44.
Le Rozier Tel: 04 65 62 60 89

Canoe Hire and rafting

There are lots of canoe hire operators - too many to list - offering a variety of short and long trips. Expect to pay about 15 euros for a half day, or 23 euros for a full day trip - please refer to our Suppliers Directory, local tourist offices, or the webbsite.

Other rivers

le Tarnon, Dourbie and Jonte are tributaries of the Tarn that offer class 4 "creek style" kayaking when water levels are sufficient, perhaps in early summer?

The Haut Tarn

Upstream of Florac the upper Tarn is totally different in character - with short sections offering some challenging class 5 and 6 paddling - steep granite rapids and big waterfalls that you may have seen featured in magazine articles. This needs good water levels after one or two days of good rain, normally best in Nov-Dec. The most famous section is from *Le Pont de Montvert* to the *la Vernede* - 10.5 km of class 5(6). You would be wise to seek advice from local paddlers if interested.

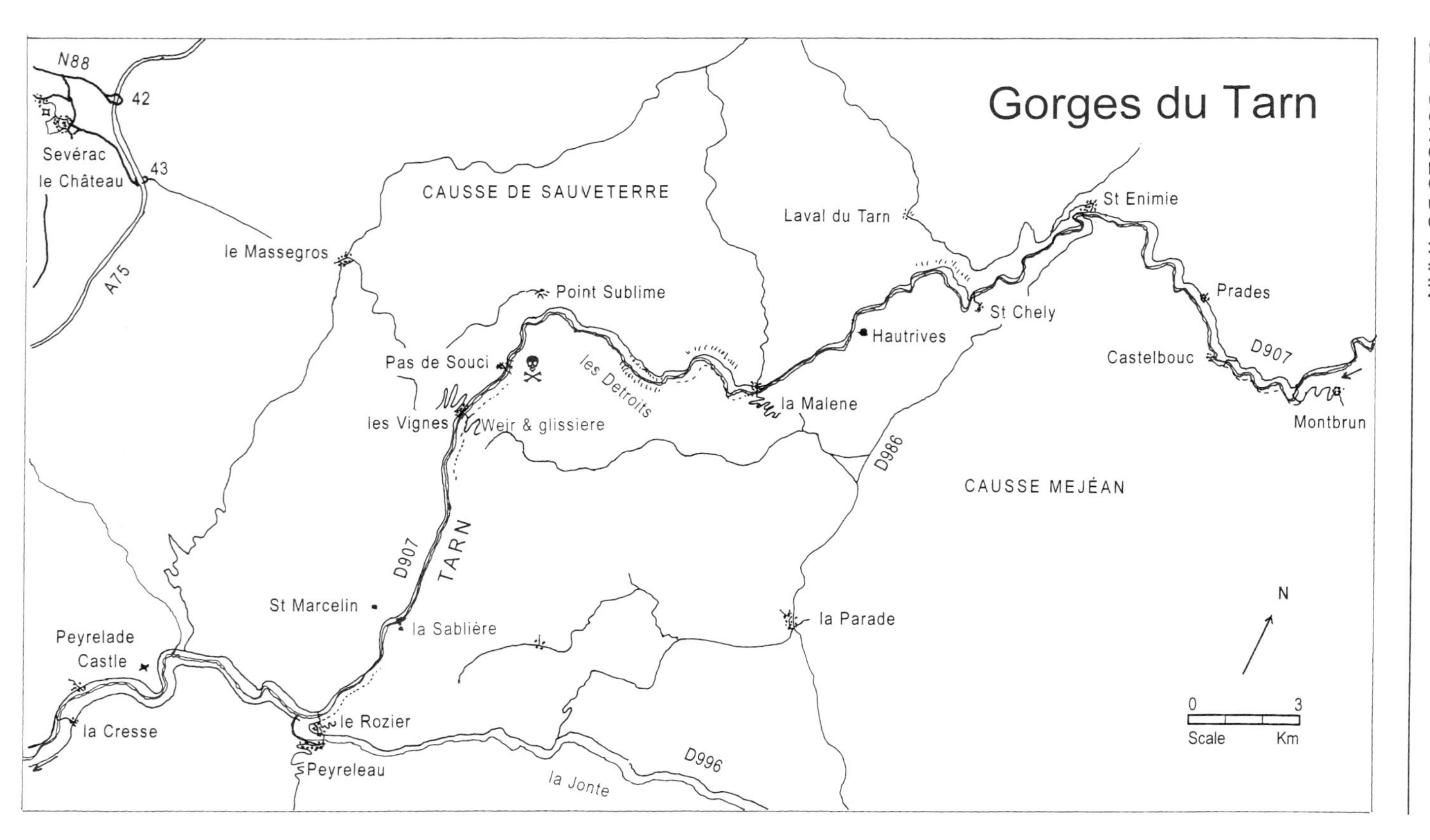
Gorges du Tarn
N88
42
43
Sevérac
le Château
A75
le Massegros
CAUSSE DE SAUVETERRE
Laval du Tarn
St Enimie
Point Sublime
St Chely
Prades
Hautrives
Castelbouc
D907
Pas de Souci
les Detroits
la Malene
Montbrun
les Vignes
Weir & glissiere
D986
CAUSSE MEJÉAN
TARN
D907
St Marcelin
la Sablière
la Parade
N
Peyrelade
Castle
0
3
Scale
Km
le Rozier
la Cresse
D996
Peyreleau
la Jonte

le Pont du Tarn to Montbrun **18km of class 2-3** ★★ ❁❁ -

Water quality - OK. Temperature - warm Busy? <50

Water levels are often too low for this section in high summer.

Put in at by the old bridge at Pont du Tarn at the confluence of the Tarn and Tarnon. This is the top part of the Gorges where the valley sides are less steep and the river flows in a wider valley bottom, so there are gravel beds which make for bump and scrape at low levels. In spring or early summer the run is described as pleasantly scenic and it has some eight or so rapids that might rate a class 3 in higher water levels. There are no weirs or other special hazards.

Montbrun to Sainte Enimie **10km of class 1-2** ★ ❁❁ ☺☺

Water quality - OK. Temp. - warm. 5 cumecs? Busy? <50

Put in on the left bank 500m upstream from the bridge. There are lots of small rapids and riffles, quite technical, and a fast current, so you do need to concentrate a little and cannot just bumble down looking at the scenery, which is all very impressive, and a foretaste of what is to come. Most of the rapids are shallow and when the river is low paddlers sometimes build little dams to channel the water.

Castelbouc is a wonderful little village on the river left after 3.5 km, with ancient houses built into the overhanging cliffs, and a ruined castle perched on a pinnacle above. This is well worth a little stroll ashore (and perhaps an ice cream?). Note well the concrete bridge that is 500m upstream of the village - this only has some 60cm of headroom at low water so could be dangerous at high flows.

Gorges du Tarn - the village of Castelbouc. *Eric Knowles*

One kilometre down the river brings you to the village of **Prades** and a concrete dam. Either portage left, or in low water slide the boats down the dam on the left - the main flow goes down a grill and fish pass on the right. Easy water then takes you down to the mini slalom course and 'Centre Plein Air' above Sainte Enimie.

Portage the weir at **Sainte Enimie** on the left. This is one of the main canoe hire centres and is impressively busy as it is the main tourist centre for the valley

Sainte Enimie to La Malene **14 km of class 1-2** ★★ ❀❀❀ ☺☺

Water quality - OK. Temp. - warm 8 cumecs? Busy? <200

This is the real start of the 'Gorges du Tarn' and from here the views get better with every bend of the river as the canyon narrows and the cliffs rise ever higher.

The usual put in is on the river right just above the bridge. 200m below the bridge is a class 2 rapid where the current runs left onto some rocks. When we were there, the canoe hire companies had erected a prominent 'Danger' sign to try and protect their canoes.

St Chely du Tarn is after about 4 km and is justly renowned as a picturesque old village, with the houses huddled in the cliffs of the *'Cirque de Chely'*. An underground stream comes spouting out of the foundations of the village and cascades into the river. Land on the left above the bridge if you wish to explore. There is a picnic site just below the church and this could make a pleasant put in or take out.

The river then bends left under the magnificent *'Cirque de Pougnadoires'* and small rapids continue. The *Chateau la Caze* on the right is now a rather splendid luxury hotel where scruffy river runners aren't that welcome, but another 2km brings you to the attractive ruined hamlet of **Hautrives** on the river left. Here there is a friendly, low key, café in the gardens of one of the semi-ruined houses. This attractive little village can only be reached by a combination of footpath, canoe or aerial runway and it is being restored with the help of EEC funds. Note the ruined castle perched on a seemingly inaccessible pinnacle, high above the village.

Just below the village is a bouncy little rapid that might be class 2 and then the river quietens down as it approaches the barrage at **la Malene**. Portage or slide your boat over the barrage on the river left and then land on the beach on the right above the bridge.

Merganser duck

La Malene to Pas du Souci	**10 km of class 1**	★★★	❀❀❀	☺☺
Water quality - OK.	Temp. - warm. 8 cumecs?		Busy?	>200

Summary

This is the most scenic and also the easiest part of the Gorges so very popular and very busy in high season. On this stretch of the river keep your eyes open behind so that you don't get run over by one of the big heavy punts of 'les Bateliers'.

> **Fluffy's Top Tip:**
> Most of the hire boats are on the water between 1000 and 1700 hours so try to paddle this early morning or evening, when you should pretty much have the river to yourself - there were no restrictions on paddling hours at the time of writing.

Description

La Malene is a pleasant village with bars and restaurants, so no hardship if you have to wait for the shuttle. Note that if you are starting here you can drive down to the beach to unload through the car park on the right bank above the bridge.

After a couple of kilometres the gorge narrows and becomes a box canyon - the cliffs soar until they seem to reach straight from the river to the sky - this is **'les Detroits'** (the Narrows) and the very heart of the gorge. There are some beautiful white beaches and deep pools nestling in the cliffs which beckon for a picnic and a swim in this idyllic spot. The rapids are little more than riffles and it's very pleasant just to float and admire the scenery and admire the numerous schools of fish that glide in the transparent waters under your boat .

As you come out of the narrows, the tall cliffs of the *'Cirque des Baumes'* face you on the right, and on both sides of the river there are fantastic shaped, multi-coloured pinnacles framing the sky line. A few small rapids maintain the paddling interest and one, where the river flows under a bit of an undercut on the left, is signed, and might even be class 2 in some water levels.

Take out on the beach approximately 500m before the **Pas de Souci** - we strongly recommend that you scout this out in advance on the shuttle so that you will recognise it from the river (note that different canoe hire companies have different take outs). If you wish to continue on the river you will need to portage along the road for nearly a kilometre - then from here to Les Vignes is less than a kilometre of mainly flat water.

The Pas de Souci

This a chaos of massive rock blocks that have fallen from the cliffs above so that the river now has to flow through and under this convoluted syphon. For 20 francs you can climb up the stairs to a viewing platform overlooking the river and visualise the nightmare scenario what would happen if you missed the take out! There have been several fatalities here and there is a memorial to a German who died in 1981, but whose body parts were only recovered four months later.

les Vignes to le Rozier	**10 km of class 2 (3-)**	★★★ ❁❁❁ ☺
Water quality - OK.	Temp. - warm. 10 cumecs?	Busy? <200

Summary

This is the best section if you are looking for wild water and wild scenery. The French call this *"très sportive et amusant"* which gives you a nice feel for the paddling and you will certainly get quite wet in an open canoe. Most of the rapids are bedrock rapids, with big boulders that need some manoeuvring, some quite "whooshy" shoots, and wave trains. We noticed that there didn't seem to be too many rental canoes on this section but there is though, usually sufficient water for rafting and you can also hire inflatable canoes, which are called 'hot dogs'.

The valley appears wilder than it actually is - for most of the way all you can see is the river ahead of you, wooded valley sides and the escarpment cliffs on the sky line marking the canyon rim. There are very few houses, and the road is hidden in the trees, well above and away from the river. Griffin Vultures were nesting and soaring on the escarpment and a massive buzzard swooped down and landed on a tree a few metres ahead of our boat - we could have been in Canada!

Description

At les **Vignes** there is a high sloping weir with a superb, adrenaline-pumping, 'glissiere', so you can either put in at the car park on the river right above, or start below. The faint-hearted should note that although this glissiere looks spectacular and is quite photogenic, it's actually easier than it looks at first sight!

There's a rafting and canoe hire base about a kilometre below the village with a high ropes course and bodies flying across the river above your head on aerial runways. About 500m below is a cave and resurgent hidden in trees on the left. After this, its a bit more peaceful with just you, the river, and the gorge. There are plenty of rapids to provide entertainment - most are where the river has carved into the limestone bedrock, but none are unduly difficult. In places the bank has been undercut by the current, and there are a few undercut boulders, so this is not a section for the beginner and you should take reasonable care.

About 5 km downstream is *le 'Petit Pas de Souci'* - only a very tame version of its big brother, where some huge blocks of rock have fallen off the cliffs and created small rapids and some fun eddies.

The small village of **la Sabliere** is about half way down the river and the aerial runway that crosses to it, upsteam of the village, marks the infamous **'Sabliere' rapid**, which is the most difficult one on the river - usually an easy class 3. If you have any doubts and/or have an expensive boat, you might want to scout this. Still water follows below and allows rescue and salvage.

About 300m below there is a rafting ramp on the right and then about 200m further on is another 'whooshy' rapid with a fine wave train - a class 2+ or 3-.

Continuing down the river, the scenery remains excellent - after the next bend take a look back upstream at the ruined 'troglodyte village of *St Marcelin'* high up in cliffs on the right. About a kilometre above le Rozier is a rafting base on the right bank which offers a welcome ice cream stop, and then the usual take out at **le Rozier** is the public beach on the right just downstream of the bridge.

rn - 'la Sablière' rapid below les Vignes.

Célé - setting off from Brengues.

Lot - 'la Digue' play wave below Entraygues.
Sue Richardson

Fluffy trying to stay dry.

ɔt - riverside château at Entraygues.

Célé - stopping for ice creams at Espagnac.

Le Rozier to la Cresse	**10 km of class 1-2 (2+)**	★	❁❁	☺
Water quality - OK.	Temp. - warm. 15 cumecs?		Busy? <200	

Summary

This section is a little bit of an anticlimax after the splendours of what has gone before, but still a fine paddle in a beautiful valley - wide, with well-wooded valley sides and fringed by high cliffs on the skyline. The river is wide with gravel bars forming straight-forward class 1-2 rapids with just the odd boulder and obvious lines, so this makes a good training run for aspiring white water paddlers.

Jack Pease says: "The most dangerous part of this run is perhaps the swimming kids - they sometimes dive bomb your boat from the cliffs!"

Description

For the first few km there are many pleasant campsites in the meadows alongside the river on the right bank and the magnificent ruins of **Peyrelad Castle** are prominent on the skyline downstream. Just above Peyreleau village, about 4km down the river, there are the remains of a weir next to an old mill - this forms a class 2+ shoot and a fine play wave. We recommend taking out at the bridge at **la Cresse**, downstream on the left bank *. The river downstream becomes progressively less scenic, flat (class 1), and has several weirs that require portaging, but is described as pleasant for canoe-camping as far as **Avalats**, another 87 km.

If you continue past la Cresse note that there is a potentially dangerous rapid just a few hundred yards downstream that should be run on the right as the left route leads into a nasty boulder garden.

Gorges du Tarn, 'la Sabliere' rapid. *Sue Richardson*

Les Bateliers de Malene

I can remember as a small boy, coming to the Gorges du Tarn on a family camping holiday and being punted down the river by a swarthy boatman in a grey beret - the very archetype of how I imagined a Frenchman. On the calm sections he would casually pull out and light a strong, stomach-wrenching cigarette, point out the landmarks and in guttural French tell gory stories of ancient battles. I was thrilled at the way he so effortlessly guided us down the river and for the next three months my dreams of being a fighter pilot changed to becoming a French boatmen!

Ever since the 19th Century the Bateliers de Malene have been carrying tourists down the river through the deepest and narrowest part of the gorge. They use a simple flat-bottomed punt that holds 6 passengers and the boatman poles this through the rapids. My childhood dreams were sadly shattered when I discovered that these days the boatmen have a quiet little 4 cylinder outboard engine for the flat stretches between the rapids, there is no time for a quick fag - what used to take half a day now takes an hour so they can get many more trips in the day and make lots more money. (If you are interested, trips cost about 17 euros a head and can be booked through the Tourist Office)

The Millau White Water Course

The new white water course at Millau is somewhere in size between the Nottingham and Northampton ones and is probably better than both. It consists of a nearly straight descent of 400 metres through about half-a -dozen single drop rapids. Characteristics are varied using movable plastic flow modifiers (the same French system that was chosen for the Sydney Olympics) and by adjusting the volume of flow down the course - 5-20 cumecs, depending on the river level and entry sluice angle.

At about 10 cumecs (sluice full open with 'summer' river level) the rapids give the impression of being mostly benign, but even at this level (roughly a grade 2) they have some surprises in store. They are variable in difficulty, so you can pick your spot, developing skills at your own pace. Particularly good fun is a large glassy standing wave right in the middle of one exit; get on it (if you can!) and you can scoot from side to side just using tiny weight shifts.

The course has a good mixture of play spots , with generous still and recirculating eddies. Each pool basin has plenty of re-entry points, but be prepared to remove some plastic on the rough surfaces during seal launches. You can regain the start easily (at least a lowish water level) by rejoining the Tarn, portaging a low partly dry weir and then flat-water paddling a short distance to above the entry sluice. Alternatively, lug your boat up the path to the top-pool entry ramp.

The course is fed by the Tarn so the water us is reasonably clean and it should be paddleable (at least straight through) by anyone with a little white water experience, and it is reasonably safe and friendly inasmuch as there is not much for swimmers to wallop as they go down the rapids. Road access is good, parking plentiful, the staff are very friendly and it's cheap (£2 for a day ticket). Kayaks (including some interesting demo boats) and inflatables can be hired.

by Mansur Darlington

Arrh, Mum ...! Filming in the Gorges du Tarn.

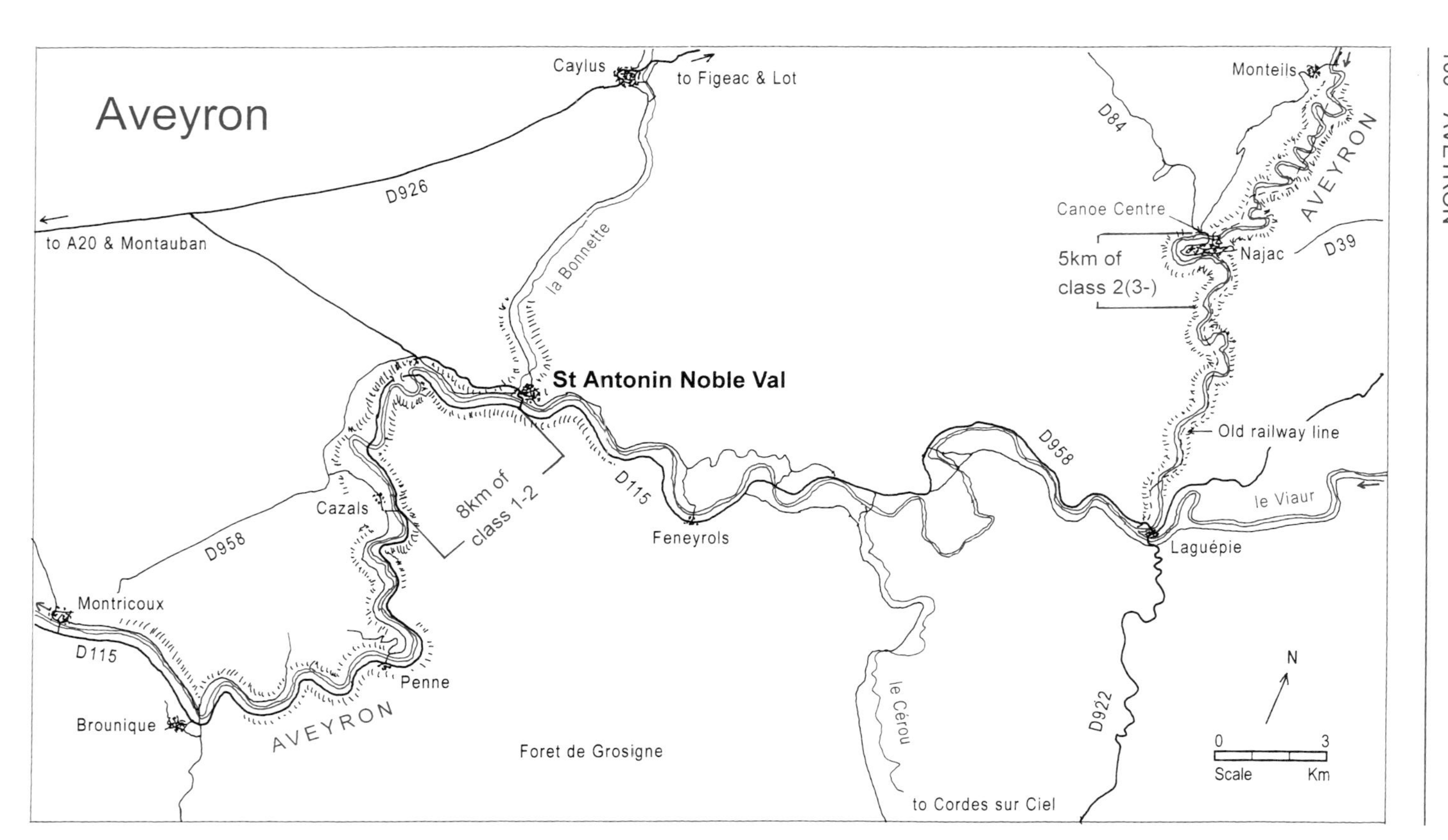
Aveyron
Caylus
to Figeac & Lot
D926
to A20 & Montauban
la Bonnette
St Antonin Noble Val
8km of class 1-2
D115
Feneyrols
Cazals
D958
Montricoux
D115
Penne
Brounique
AVEYRON
Foret de Grosigne
le Cérou
to Cordes sur Ciel
D922
Monteils
D84
AVEYRON
Canoe Centre
5km of class 2(3-)
Najac
D39
Old railway line
D958
le Viaur
Laguépie
N
0 3
Scale Km

Aveyron

From information supplied by Graham Bland and others.

Summary

Gorges du Najac	2 (3-)	5	★	❁	☺	<50	Short fun run.
St Antonin to Cazals	1-2	8	★	❁❁	☺	<50	Scenic run with good beaches.

Two short stretches with pleasant gorge scenery and easy rapids. Worth considering if you are in the area.

The River

The Aveyron is sandwiched between the better known valleys of the Lot, to the North, and the Tarn to the South and shares similar characteristics. The river runs West, from close to the Cevennes, through the Aveyron region, eventually joining the Tarn just North of Montauban.

While much of the rivers route is across rolling French countryside, between Villefranche-de-Rouergue and Najak it cuts an impressive limestone gorge and then another one west of St Antonin.

During the summer months, paddling is limited to the two sections discussed here – but earlier in the year, water levels open up longer stretches, particularly North of Najac.

Off the river

There are many fortified 'Bastide' villages in the area, built in the aftermath of the persecutions, Najac, Penne, Montricoux, Brunique are all fine examples. The most famous (and touristy) is Cordes-sur-Ciel – a picturesque 12th century town of cobbled streets spiralling up a 70 metres high peak, (hence its name 'in the sky'). Lots of artists workshops, traditional local craft, boutiques and restaurants here.

St Antonin-Noble-Val is worth a visit, particularly on Sunday mornings – when the market draws people in from all around to stock up on largely locally grown fruit and vegetables, excellent cheeses, wine, foie gras, honey etc.

The Oak forest (Foret de Gresigne) just to the South of the Gorges L'Aveyron provides for some good walking and mountain-biking. While this forest is managed by the National Forestry Office it is home to a substantial population of deer and wild-boar.

There are various lakes in the region - the lake at Monclar offers safe swimming, waterslides, sandy beaches, diving platform. There's also horse-riding, trekking, climbing, pot-holing, and a couple of golf-courses in the area.

Food and drink

Plenty of small café's and restaurants in the area – but you can't beat a baguette and bottle of local wine on a river beach in the sunshine

Camping

There's a pleasant, riverside campsite at Narjac at the put in of the run - 'Municipal le Paiserou', tel: 05 65 29 73 96.

Maps and Guides

IGN Top 100 sheet 57 covers the Aveyron, lower Lot, and Célé at a scale of 1:100,000 so is a good buy.

Tourist Offices

Najac, tel: 05 65 29 72 05 www.najac.com
St Antonin Noble Val, tel: 05 63 30 63 47

Canoe Hire and rafting

Several companies in both Najac and St Antonin - please see local tourist offices for a full list. We recommend the Canoe-Kayak Club de Najak, situated at the camp-site on the river (well signed) – which provides a friendly efficient service.

Other rivers

The Gorges du Viaur is a dam controlled tributary of the Aveyron but there appears to be no water releases or paddling on it in the summer months, We couldn't find any canoe hire companies and were unable to paddle or check this out, however it looks very scenic and appeared to have enough water to paddle it when we were there in late-August. Less problematical are the Célé and the Lot which are just over an hour's drive away.

The younger generation, in their flat boats, looked on in awe as Eric went airborne - "radical" they thought, "Is this the way that playboats will go?"

Gorges du Najac	**5km of class 2 (3-)**	★	❁	☺
Water quality - o.k.	Temperature - warm		Busy? <50	

Summary

Sold by local companies as the 'Mini Tour of Najak', this is a very short run through the gorges around Najak (class 2). with plenty of small rapids the whole way down. Good scenery and quiet when compared to other rivers.

Description

The put in is at the campsite on the left bank in Najac. Main features of the descent are:

1 There's one chute (with eight or ten salmon steps) that is not advisable for young children even at very low levels – but very easily portaged (and can be easily protected for older paddlers).
2 A natural weir with a surfable wave - and good picnic beach).
3 A small slalom course – pool drop, about 200m+ long which provides a great 'training ground' for learners.

A rough road follows the river all the way to the take out just below the Slalom Course The river levels dropped appreciably while we were there and by the end-August they were too low (although groups were still paddling). Najak itself is worth a visit – a medieval hill-top village with a castle and a few good restaurants.

Below this section, from the confluence with the Viuar, the river is flat, with many weirs and it runs in a wide valley until St Antonin.

St Antonin to Cazals	**8km of class 1-2**	★	❁❁	☺
Water quality - o.k.	Temperature - warm		Busy? <50	

Summary

This is the main tourist run on the Aveyron through the Gorges to Cazals and it provides an easy and scenic canoe with long lines of limestone cliffs similar to the river Lot or Célé.

Description

A road follows the river closely and makes for an easy shuttle but detracts from the experience a little. However there are plenty of beaches along the way for swimming and sun bathing. There's a beach bar at the take out at Cazals for ice creams and cold beers – situated next to a chute with a small 'play wave'.

The gorges continue for 7km from Cazals to Penne but this section was closed when we were there, reportedly because of fallen trees in the chutes. Alternatively, you can extend the day with a flat paddle by putting in at Fenyrols, some 7 km upstream of St Antonin.

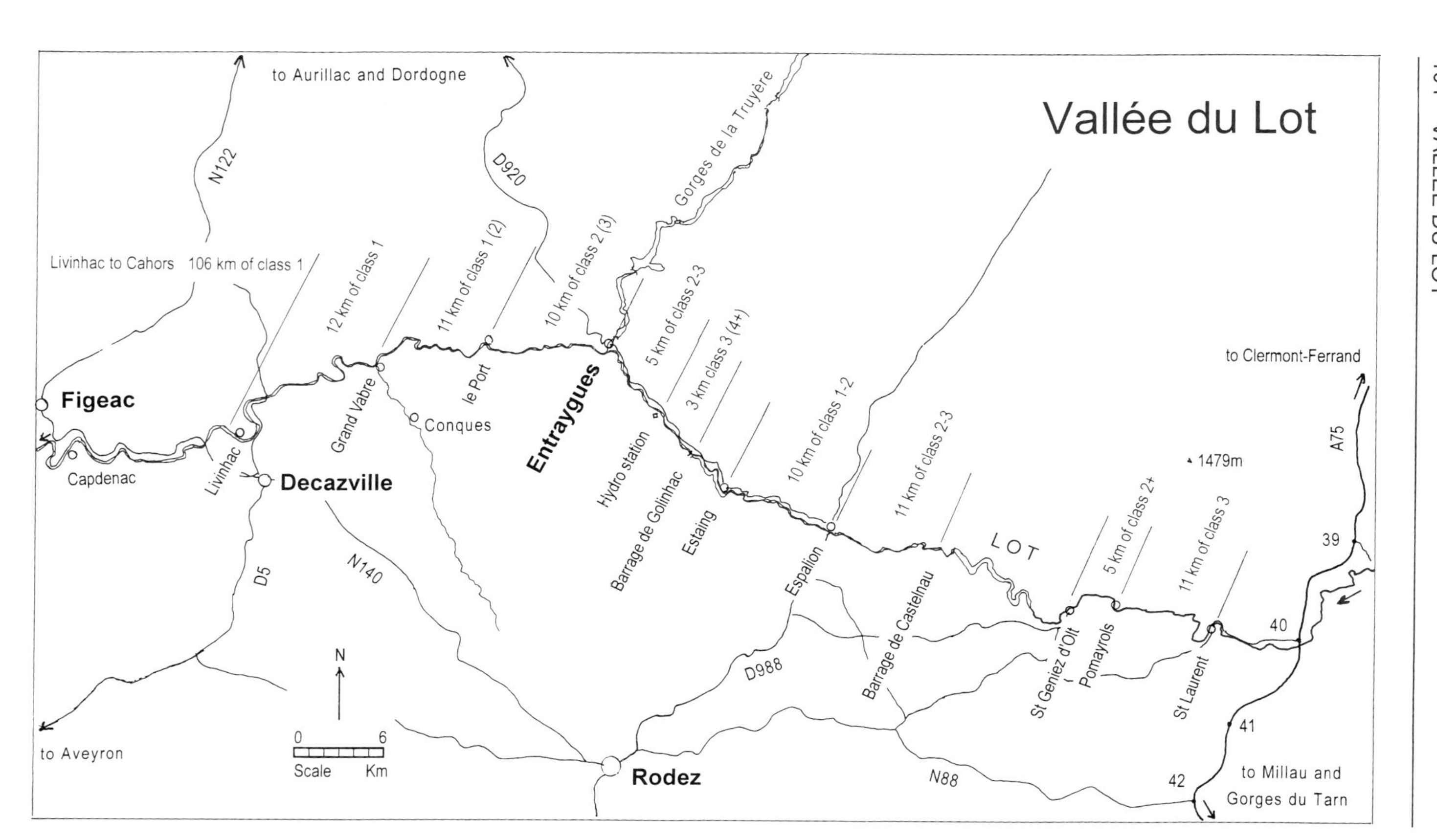
Vallée du Lot
to Aurillac and Dordogne
N122
D920
Gorges de la Truyère
Livinhac to Cahors 106 km of class 1
12 km of class 1
11 km of class 1 (2)
10 km of class 2 (3)
5 km of class 2-3
3 km class 3 (4+)
10 km of class 1-2
11 km of class 2-3
5 km of class 2+
11 km of class 3
1479m
to Clermont-Ferrand
A75
39
40
41
42
Figeac
Capdenac
Livinhac
Decazville
Grand Vabre
Conques
le Port
Entraygues
Hydro station
Barrage de Golinhac
Estaing
Espalion
LOT
Barrage de Castelnau
St Geniez d'Olt
Pomayrols
St Laurent
D5
N140
D988
N88
N
0
6
Scale
Km
Rodez
to Aveyron
to Millau and
Gorges du Tarn

Lot

Summary

River and run	Class	Km	Stars	Scen.	Fluffy	Busy	Notes
St Laurent to Pom.>	3	11	★★★	❁❁	-	<10	*Usually insufficient water in Jul Aug.*
Pomayrols to St Gn.	2+	5	★★	❁❁	☺	<50	Tight gorge & fun playboating spot.
Barrage to Espalion>	2-3	11	★★	❁	-	<10	*Usually insufficient water in Jul-Aug.*
Espalion to Estaing	1-2	14	★	❁	☺	<10	*Usually insufficient water in Jul-Aug.*
Barrage to Hydro plant	3(4+)	3	★★	❁	-	<10	*Usually insufficient water in Jul-Aug.*
Hydro plant to Entrgs>	2-3	5	★★	❁❁	-	<10	*Usually insufficient water in Jul-Aug.*
Entraygues to Port	2(3-)	10	★★	❁❁	☺	<50	Classic run.
le Port to Grnd Vabre	1 (2)	11	★★	❁❁	☺☺	<50	Friendly, ideal beginners run.
Grand Vabre to Livinc	1	12	★	❁❁	☺	<10	2 weirs
Livinhac to Cahors	1	106	★	❁❁	-	<10	Scenic canoe touring but many weirs

A green unspoilt heavily wooded valley which winds through the plateau and hills of the Massif Central. The river Lot has a pleasant variety of paddling and many magnificent ancient towns and villages along its banks. The whole area is relatively unspoilt and undiscovered by mass tourism.

The River

I have vague memories of a trip to France with the Canoe Camping Club way back in the 1960's. After the Dordogne and the Tarn, a few of us stayed on and wondered what to do next. We looked at a map and saw this river called the Lot so decided to drive to it to see what it was like. I remember how delighted we were to discover this beautiful unspoilt river - and some 30 years later I was equally delighted and a little surprised to find that the Vallée du Lot is much the same - quiet, undiscovered and beautiful.

The Lot rises close to the sources of the Tarn and the Allier, and then sweeps westwards nearly 500km to join the Garonne. The Truyère is a major tributary which joins at Entraygues but which is spoilt for canoeing by a whole series of hydro dams.. For most of the upper river the Lot flows through the rolling countryside of Aveyron where the the steep sided wooded valley is pastoral, green, and pretty rather than spectacular. Then in its middle stretches, the river cuts through the limestone plateau of Quercy in a beautiful, sinuous, meandering canyon, similar to the Dordogne. The name 'Lot' is reversed in the local patois (langue d'Oc) to become 'Olt' so many of the place names in the upper valley incorporate this - e.g. St Geniez d'Olt.

Undoubtedly beautiful - however, no one has ever called the Lot "spectacular" and this has probably been its saviour. The Ardèche and Tarn are famous for their magnificent gorges. The Dordogne has perhaps become too fashionable for its own good, despite the beauty of its historic towns, and its fine cuisine. The Lot has just quietly enjoyed NOT being famous, and this is very much to its advantage - if you are looking for a scenic centre for a paddling holiday away from the crowds then this has to be one of our top recommendations!

Hannah Paul wrote - "Barbara and I got on really well with the kayaks on this lovely section of the Lot river, doing more stuff than we had down in the cooler waters of the UK. The lost valley of the Lot has a certain 'caught in time' air to it - we enjoyed the freedom, weather, and scenery so much so that we forgot about going on to the Ardèche and had one of our best holidays ever."

Water levels are often too low to paddle in the upper river by high summer, but there are often unpredictable releases from the Barrage de Canstelnau upstream of Espalion, often in the afternoons - we suggest enquiring at one of the canoe bases.

Canoe Camping

This is a classic river for the canoe-camper with the most popular section being the 150km from Entraygues to Cahors - class 1 and 2 in a beautiful scenic valley with un-crowded campsites, and interesting old villages to explore. Even in the height of summer, when water levels are at their lowest, there is adequate water in this section. The only negative point is that the lower river (below Livinhac) has a lot of weirs on it which require portaging and this is probably the main reason why it is not as popular as the Dordogne, its rival to the North.

Off the river

Many magnificent ancient towns and villages just cry out to be explored. Conques, Entraygues, Estaing, are just a few that are a delight to wander around. Estaing has a medieval fete on the first Sunday in July. The main town of the valley is Espallion and is an excellent tourist venue, with an interesting diving museum.

Mountain biking is a bit limited here because of the deep and narrow valley but there are some scenic routes up on the plateau and very pleasant cycling along the upper valley around Espalion. Canyoning is also possible. Ask the local tourist office for information leaflets on any of these activities.

Food and drink

The speciality of the Region is 'Aligot' and one of the best places to try this is every Friday night in the fine family run inn and restaurant *'Chez Marie'* in **Grand Vabre**.

In **Entraygues** the salad bar on the tree-shaded main square is good value and *'La Truyère'* near the old bridge is a family run hotel and restaurant that can be recommended. The *Aux Arms* in **Estaing** overlooks the river, and offers superb provincial cooking at reasonable prices. The landlady likes to practice her English and will translate the menu.

Peter Thorn recommends the *'Ferme Auberge de Mesanjerie'* which is worth a visit for a special occasion. Follow the road from Entraygues towards Laguiole (pronounced Layol) for 4 km. A substantial six-course meal with wine will cost about 25 euros each. The main course is cooked on a spit over a wood fire. He says "to allow 2½ hours and wear loose clothing"!. Book by phone; details from the Tourist Office in Entraygues. The *'Ferme Auberge de Batadou'* is a similar restaurant that can be recommended for good local food and also has a gite and camping.

Beaulieu - a cultural quest for ice creams.

Camping

There is a good selection of riverside campsites up and down the valley. The municipal campsite in **Entraygues** *'Val de Saures'* is beautifully and conveniently sited on the riverside, well set up, and good value. There is an indoor pool, and the town's café's and bars are within easy staggering distance - tel: 05 65 44 56 92 .

The riverside campsite below le Port, *Camping Coursavy* is popular with foreign kayakers tel: 04 71 49 97 70 email campimg.cousavy@wanadoo.fr. Another riverside site, but on the Dourbie, is *Camping de Moulin* which is a more typical friendly French site, can be highly recommended.

For **cottage hire**, spring to the end of September, Peter Thorn recommends Liz Reid (Tel: 0033 565 44 5276). She manages ten quality cottages, most with pools, sleeping between 4 and 8, in the Entraygues area.

Maps and Guides

IGN Top 100 sheet 58 covers the upper and middle Lot and also the Tarn at a scale of 1:100,000 so is a good buy. Sheet 57 covers the lower Lot, Célé and Aveyron.

The 'Guide Canoe-Kayak 'la Descente du Lot' covers the whole 480km of the river and is available from Le Canotier, main tourist information offices, and canoe hire bases for approx. 7 euros. The Michelin Green guide to Dordogne, Berry and Limousin has an excellent section on the 'Basse Vallée du Lot'.

Tourist Offices

Espallion, tel: 05 65 44 10 63
Entraygues, tel: 05 65 44 56 10
Figeac, tel: 05 65 34 06 25 www.quercy.net/figeac
Cahors, tel: 05 65 53 26 30 www.tourisme-lot.com

Canoe Hire

St Geniez d'Olt, ADALPA,
tel: 05 65 70 47 84 email: adalpa@wanadoo.fr
Entraygues & Vieillevie, Association Sportive de la Vallée d'Olt
tel: 04 71 49 95 81 email: asvolt.canoe@wanadoo.fr
Larnagol, Balad's Canoe,
tel: 05 65 30 21 31.
St Cirq Lapopie, Kalapca,
Tel: 05 65 30 29 51
Bouzies, and **Albas** Safaraid, www.canoe-dordogne.com
tel: 05 65 30 74 47 email: safaraid@aol.com

Other rivers

The main tributary of the Lot is the Truyère, but this is completely dammed for Hydro schemes and is now just a series of sterile reservoirs and huge concrete dams. However, the Célé, Gorges du Tarn, and Dordogne are only a few hours drive and offer a wide variety of paddling. The Gorges de l'Aveyron to the south west are also a possibility for family canoeing.

The upper reaches of the Lot, around Mende offers some 60km of technical paddling, mainly class 2 and 3 when there is sufficient water - normally outside the summer months. The Boroalde stream above Espalion offer class 3 creeking after times of heavy rain.

St Laurent to Pomayrols	**11 km of class 3**	★★★	❁❁	-
Water quality -OK.	Temperature - cool		Busy?	<10

Usually insufficient water in July and August

Peter Thorn describes this as *'a fine trip in a steeply wooded, rocky valley and for long stretches there is no sign of human interference or influence'*. This is a wild gorge and the road is a long way off - so plan for a self-sufficient mini expedition. In low water the rapids run over sharp bedrock ledges and this make it a difficult and damaging run at these levels, and best avoided. It is usually best from April to June - check levels with the canoe base at St Geniez tel: 05 65 70 47 84. Put in at the municipal campsite (pleasant, very simple, quiet, and cheap) about a km below the pretty village of St Laurent (where there is also a pleasant, cheap hotel and restaurant). Take out on the right downstream of Pomayrols bridge - or why not continue to St Geniez?

Pomayrols to St Geniez d'Olt	**5 km of class 2+**	★★	❁❁	☺
Water quality - OK.	Temperature - cool		Busy?	<50

This is a fun section for play boat **kayaking**, even in low water levels. Put in at Pomayrols bridge. The river here has cut a 3km long narrow gorge with bedrock slabs making tight little rapids and some fine endo spots (something like the Conway or the North Esk). This section is used a lot for kayak instruction by the canoe base at St Geniez.

After this, there is a km of flat water up to 4m straight drop barrage of St Pierre. Portage left next to the fish ladder. Then it's flat and class 1 down to the canoe base and campsite just upstream of **St Geniez d'Olt** - another delightful old market town with many picturesque medieval houses.

Grand Vabre

St Geniez to Barrage de Castelnau 20 km of Hydro Reservoir

In fact, there's a weir in the centre of the town, which needs portaging and then 3 km of shallow class 1 to the little village of **St Eulalie d'Olt** where the reservoir starts - perhaps an ideal short safe introduction to river canoeing for nervous beginners?

Barrage de Castelnau to Espalion **11 km of class 2-3** ★ ❁ -

Water quality - OK. Temperature - cool Busy? <10

Usually insufficient water in July and August

A pleasant stretch if there is sufficient water. **St Come d'Olt** and **Espalion** both have riverside campsites and are picturesque old villages that are well worth exploring. Espalion has a fine 11th Century bridge with views of the medieval tannery houses that overhang and line the riverside.

Espalion to Estaing **14 km of class 1-2** ★ ❁ ☺

Water quality - OK. Temperature - cool Busy? <10

Usually insufficient water in July and August

Put in on the right below the weir in Espalion and then after 2 km look out for another weir at *St Pierre*, portage right. There is a riverside campsite 2 km above Estaing at *Hauterive* on the right. Just upstream of Estaing is another weir (the 'playwave' - see below) that may be shot in the centre if water levels permit. **Estaing** is another picturesque old town dominated by the walls of the powerful Chateau d'Estaing.

Mansur Darlington writes: *'This stretch of river combined the variations of water level that seem to characterise these reaches of the Lot in late Summer: gently sloping shingle beaches and water so shallow that 'hand-walking' is the only remedy for the heftier paddler (or those laden down with picnics and bottles) to more sporting sections where the water flow and pulse-rate rise simultaneously as the river is squeezed through a single narrowed channel. These short 'heart-starters' were frequently followed by deep clear pools, always demanding that a stop be made for a swim and iron rations.'*

Estaing to Barrage de Golinhac 5 km of Hydro Reservoir

The Play wave at Estaing.

This fine play wave is visible from the road just upstream of the village but it only works well at **high water levels** - Easter, October or Winter are normally reliable Access is easy via a riverside road, river right. This is a broken weir that forms a big cushion plus a green wave. The lake which the river flows into at Estaing needs to be a metre below maximum, with high river levels. If the lake is full, there is no wave at all, but daily discharges take effect from mid morning. This wave was the site of the French freestyle team selection event in Easter 2001. The only drawback is a hidden boulder in the run out, ready to meet any capsized head in low water.

Peter Thorn.

Barrage de Golinhac to Hydro station **3 km of class 3(4+)** ★★ ❁ -

Water quality - OK. Temperature - warm Busy? <10

Usually insufficient water.

Peter Thorn advises that this only runs sometime in **August**, when the power station is closed for maintenance and there has been some rain. A pool-drop stretch, with big boulders creating technical routes of no power, all in the heart of the 'Gorges du Lot'. At times of prolonged rain the gorge runs when the hydro cannot cope – then it can be a serious stretch with big holes and rapids joining up.

Access via track below the barrage. Egress river right before the hydro plant to a big-lay by with disused quarry hoppers.

N.B. The spillway is awesome in spate with huge spray. Some might consider it runnable but no survivors known!

Power Station to Entraygues **5 km of class 2-3.** ★★ ❁❁

Water quality - OK. Temperature - warm Busy? <10

Usually insufficient water in July and August

Water levels for this run are usually low, but rare and varied releases from the dam upstream can add up to a metre in an hour and make for a much more interesting run! Note the weir at *Méjanassère* 2 km upstream from Entraygues and scout this on your way up the valley. Also scout the take out in Entraygues where the low concrete bridge could cause problems in high water.

A 'sit on top' shooting 'la Digue' below Entraygues.

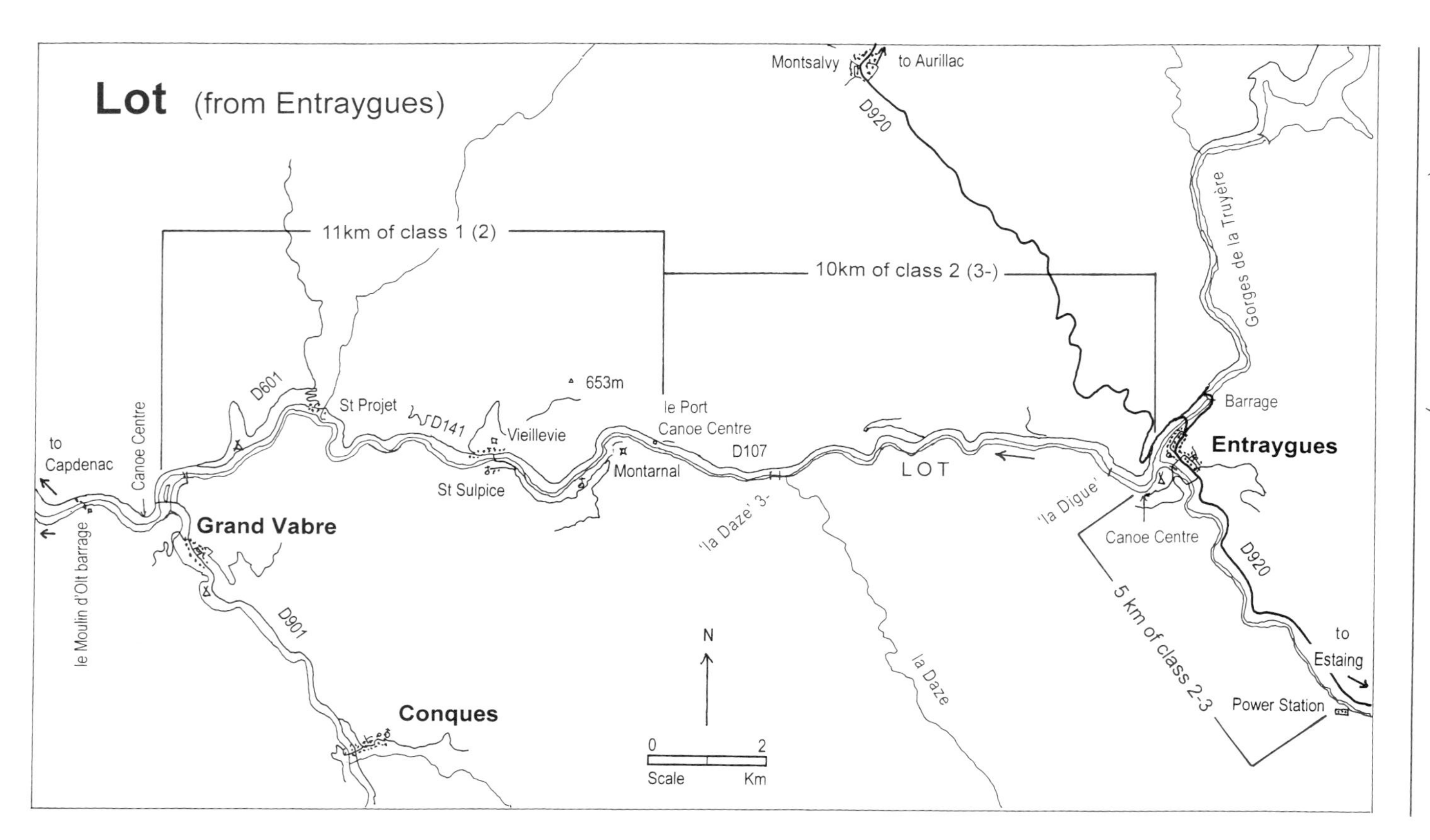
Lot (from Entraygues)
Montsalvy
to Aurillac
D920
11km of class 1 (2)
10km of class 2 (3-)
Gorges de la Truyère
Barrage
Entraygues
653m
le Port
Canoe Centre
D107
D601
St Projet
D141
Vieillevie
Montarnal
St Sulpice
to
Capdenac
Canoe Centre
LOT
'la Digue'
Canoe Centre
'la Daze' 3-
Grand Vabre
le Moulin d'Olt barrage
D920
D901
5 km of class 2-3
to
Estaing
Power Station
la Daze
N
0
2
Scale
Km
Conques

Entraygues to le Port	**10 km of class 2 (3-)**	★★	❁❁	☺
Water quality - OK.	Temperature - warm		Busy?	<50

The confluence with the river Truyère at Entraygues means that there is always sufficient water levels for paddling from here down, and this section never disappoints with a good current, some fun rapids, and beaches for lazy picnic lunches - the river flowing in a deep winding narrow, green, densely wooded valley, with the occasional views of hillside farms in the hazy distance.

There are three main canoe centres on this stretch, who work in close co-operation and offer an excellent service, and none are huge, so you will not be overwhelmed by great fleets of 'grockels' crashing and shouting their way down the river! In the summer the canoe hire companies, the Association Sportive de la Vallée d'Olt (ASVO), organise a regular shuttle bus service that returns six times a day from *Le Port*, and once a day from *Grand Vabre* - if you ask, you are normally welcome to use this service for a small charge.

Entraygues is a picturesque old town with a handsome chateau and a fine 13th century bridge over the Truyere. Put on the river just downstream from the car park in the centre or drive over the river, turn right downstream 400m, past the campsite, to put on at the Canoe School.

About one kilometre downstream brings you to a low concrete weir (about 30cm high) **'la Digue'** which has a gap in the centre that creates a fun little shoot and **play wave** in low water - good for 360's, cartwheels, etc. provided you have a short boat. The concrete weir also serves quite nicely as a picnic table for the less active!

Surfing 'la Digue'.

'A lot to remember' or 'Four have fun in France'

The trouble had really started when we'd booked the cottage in Aveyron at Easter. The owner had mentioned in passing that there were four kayaks available for use. At that point the kayaks had been of passing interest: true, we had done a pool session or two with the newly joined Frome Canoe Club, but the idea of actually canoeing on our own had little meaning. Sarah had been keen to try her hand at canoeing for years, and the boys are game for almost anything involving water. Me, well I loathe the stuff, especially when it not hot and running out of a tap, and thought I'd finally found a way of joining the family in a pool without actually getting wet. Little did I know.

But here we were, our one-star badges so new they hadn't even been sewn on, enjoying sub-tropical temperatures and a transport of delight on the upper reaches of The Lot.

Our first outing had been timid enough. We'd taken the boats to a pool we'd found earlier for swimming, just downstream of the bridge at St Come d'Olt . The pool was ideal: deep and clear, with plenty of still water but with a frisson of a flow along one bank, which made it utterly safe but interesting for an initial waterborne sortie. We had the river entirely to ourselves. Perhaps this was because it was early evening and the pubs had just opened, or perhaps it was the rolling thunder, the steel grey skies, and the forked lightning being reflected dramatically in the water. Well, we were going to get wet anyway - and, sure enough, we did.

We returned to the same spot the next day in bright sunshine and after a little practice, Sarah suggested that she would make off downstream with our two boys, and I should drive the car and meet them at a point about six kilometres away. This was the woman who only the previous day had said: "but Mansur, the water's moving. What are we supposed to do?" And now she wanted to take my heirs off into the unknown! Well, of course, they had a lovely time. I saw them about an hour later come into view round a bend in the river with their grins preceding them by about half a mile, and was soon being regaled with stories of the 'huge' rapids and 'towering' waves they had braved.

As it turned out, the choice of this stretch for our first ever sally into moving water turned out to be ideal for our limited skills. This, entirely by luck, set the pattern for the remainder of our trips on The Lot. Each stretch, selected more or less at a whim, turned out to be just right: nicely exceeding our expertise; mildly alarming; actually reasonably safe. We were encouraged that we were not being entirely irresponsible by the fact that the two local Canoe Bases, which hire out kayaks and unsinkable Canadians to the tourists, frequently take parties of children down the same stretches of river. This altered not one jot the feeling we had of being hugely adventurous, enhancing our enjoyment enormously. And who cares if the water, even at its most challenging, never exceeded grade 2.

Mansur Darlington.

Conques

There is a fair current, and small rapids all class 1, the river bends round out of sight, with green wooded valley sides, and you are surrounded by all the sounds and smells of the French countryside. There are maybe three class 2 rapids in the next 3 km, all with small waves and rocks to avoid - fun and nothing too challenging.

The main rapid and excitement is about half way down the run where a stream **'la Daze'** comes in from the left. This has formed a fine long bouncy rapid, probably an easy class 3 in low water, which will definitely get you wet - one way or another - so batten down the hatches, post the camera vultures in position, prepare for the worst and hope for the best!

After this, the next 3km seem relatively easy and bring you to another class 2 rapid at the canoe hire base at **Le Port** where there is usually a friendly welcome, ice creams, cold drinks, etc. A pleasant place to relax and play whilst you wait for the shuttle bus to run you back to Entraygues - or if you prefer, continue on another 3 km to *Vieillevie and beyond.*

Le Port to Grand Vabre	**11 km of class 1 (2)**	★★	❁❁	☺☺
Water quality - OK.	Temperature - warm		Busy? <50	

Put on at the canoe base here. One kilometre downstream is the tower of *Montarnal* high up on the opposite side, then 3 km further brings you to a class 2 rapid at the approach to the fine old village of **Vieillevie.** Take out below the bridge on the left for a look round - Vieillevie is on the famous pilgrimage route to Compostela and has a handsome 11th century chateau and several convenient bars and restaurants. The *Hotel de la Terrasse* overlooks the river, does some excellent meals, and is probably the best reason for taking out here, rather than upstream at le Port - you can egress in the field just below the hotel.

The wooded valley sides and fine scenery continues but the river has now lost a little of its sparkle for the white water paddler with mainly flat water and only a few small rapids. The canoe hire companies describe this as *'a great family trip, nice and easy, with wonderful scenery, suitable for children 5 years plus'*. French river guides use words like *'très agréable'*. How can we say more?

The little village of **St Projet** is on the right after 3 km and makes another pleasant stop for ice creams. *Camping Coursavy* is on the right after 2km, followed by the old *Pont de Coursavy* which has been superseded by a new bridge *(le Pont de Grand Vabre)* a kilometre downstream. The *Dourdou* river comes in from the left and opposite the confluence, on the right bank, is the canoe base and take out.

The pleasant village of **Grand Vabre** is a kilometre up the valley of the Dourdou. It has a fine, friendly riverside campsite *'le Moulin'* with good value pizzas. A further 5 km up the valley is the renowned unspoilt medieval town of **Conques** with its beautiful Romanesque cathedral and treasury. This was not vandalised in the French Revolution and is a 'must see' if you are in the area - we recommend that you park on the main road next to the river and walk up the steep cobbled path from here to explore this intriguing, picturesque site. Conques is one of the prime places on the famous pilgrimage route to Compostela and you will probably see several modern pilgrims following the same trail.

Super cool seal launch

Paddling clean, bouncy, grade-three through beautiful volcanic gorges in the sun is many things; fun, beautiful, and exercise, to name three, but did you know it was cool? Well it is. . .

One day Dad and me went for a paddle in our kayaks with a French friend of ours - and she brought along her daughter and one of her FRIENDS. This was in the good old days - it was a gallant and honourable time when cartwheels, hammers and such play-boating moves had yet to be invented and we poseurs had to make do with tight breakouts and fast ferry-glides, both of which I put to good use. However, one can only get so far with a young lady pretending to be a slalomist-but-cool, on grade two and in a Spud, so I decided I needed something more. Before long we rounded a bend in the river, and there it was: a giant 15 foot boulder - a superb seal launch - if it wasn't so high. The pressures were on and before I knew it I was sitting in my spud on top of this huge boulder looking over the edge - petrified!

Now at this point, any normal caring parent would have decided that 'enough is enough' and told their 13 year old, eldest son to stop being stupid and get down. But no - I sat there, a condemned man, looking hopefully down at my Dad in vain - but he just floated about at the foot of the rock shouting, "Hang on a minute", as he struggled to get out his camera. While this was happening, the two girls performed some kind of military-style pincer movement and appeared behind me on top of 'Death Rock', effectively, closing all escape routes.

Resigned to death, I instructed the girls to, "Pushe tres much". My final pause for parental reprieve was broken by Dad shouting, "Come on, Im ready" - and that was it, they started pushing and before I knew it I'd passed the balance point and the front of my boat had dropped forwards. This was OK but the next bit wasn't as the girls chose to, 'Pushe tres much' and they pushed the already vertical back of my boat outwards 'tres beaucoup much' - sending me cart wheeling through the air.

I landed with a crash - head first, upside-down, with the deck of the boat slapping down flat and stopping dead on the surface of the water. But my body carried on - my thighs were wrenched out of the braces leaving me half hanging out of my boat, upside down, feeling smashed, winded, and with my thighs killing me. Quickly I pulled myself half back in, found my paddles and rolled up, trying to put on my best 'it really didn't hurt' face.

"Great photo!" said Dad.

Later that evening I limped into town for a promised hot date with the girls and to cash-in the day's hard earned cool points - I got a lovely snog off the fit girl - and yes the fear and the pain were worth it!

Rob Taylor

Grand Vabre to Livinhac	**12 km of class 1** (2 weirs)	★	❁❁	☺
Water quality - OK.	Temperature - warm		Busy? <10	

A pleasant quieter section with fine scenery, similar in many ways to the preceding section but not as popular because of the two weirs that are usually portaged.
Starting at Grand Vabre gives you 2 km of flat lake up to the dam at the *Moulin d'Olt* - land left to scout and portage.

The river now makes two huge meanders into the surrounding hills, and after 4 km the pleasant village of **St Parthem** is on the right with a riverside campsite just upstream. 8 km brings you to the bridge at Port d'Agres. 3 km round the bend is the old mill and weir at *Marcenac*, usually portaged left. Take out at the suspension bridge at **Livinhac** on the right bank upstream.

Livinhac to Cahors	**106 km of class 1** (many weirs)	★	❁❁	-
Water quality - OK.	Temperature - warm		Busy? <50	

This is perhaps the most beautiful stretch of the river Lot as it cuts in great loops through the plateau of Quercy. The valley sides rise in steep heavily wooded slopes from the river and are surmounted by long lines of limestone cliffs gleaming white in the sunshine.

The river is quiet and pleasant with lots of fish and surprisingly friendly fisherman. Mostly flat, but with a helpful current, the only drawback is the numerous weirs - over 30 of them, which have to be inspected, and portaged or run, as appropriate. In high water these could be dangerous but in normal low water summer levels these should normally pose no major hazard. The weirs mean that this run is much less popular than say the Dordogne, and you will meet only a few other canoes.

This is a very historic stretch of the river, with a plethora of ancient, picturesque villages, reeking of history, and with many strange tales to tell. These cry out to be explored - and how better to visit them than by river, camping each night in a pleasant riverside site?

St Cirq Lapopie is a famous tourist site just before the confluence of the Célé and downstream from here the locks have been restored so you will meet the occasional pleasure boat.

Please refer to the '*Guide Canoe-Kayak 'la Descente du Lot'* for more detailed information.

Pied Wagtail

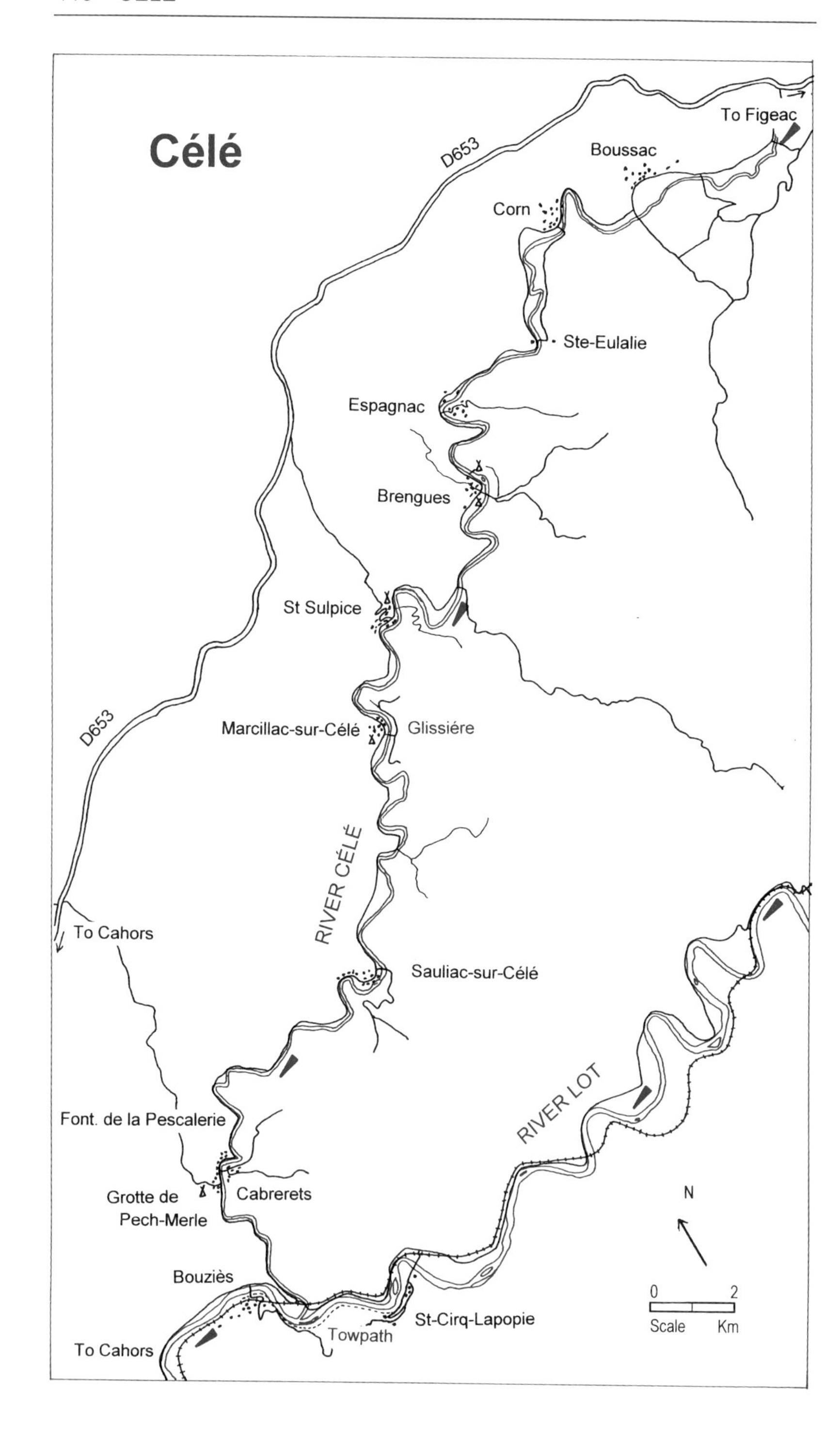
Célé
D653
To Figeac
Boussac
Corn
Ste-Eulalie
Espagnac
Brengues
St Sulpice
D653
Marcillac-sur-Célé
Glissiére
RIVER CÉLÉ
To Cahors
Sauliac-sur-Célé
RIVER LOT
Font. de la Pescalerie
Grotte de
Pech-Merle
Cabrerets
N
Bouziès
0
2
Scale
Km
St-Cirq-Lapopie
Towpath
To Cahors

Célé

Summary

Boussac to Bouzies	1 (2)	40	★	❀❀	☺☺	<50	Friendly, small, ideal family run.

French river expert Michelle Legume said to us "Tous les gens aime le Célé" - everybody likes the Célé and how right he is! Here's a friendly, easy, scenic river that is ideal for young families.

The River

The Célé valley is like some miniature version of the Lot - like its big sister it carves its way through the limestone plateau of the Causse de Gamat in a sinuous and highly picturesque canyon. The valley floor is flat and fertile so the rugged limestone cliffs, scrub and beech woods of the valley sides contrast with well tended fields of tobacco, maize, sunflowers, and vineyards. Quaint old villages are built into the cliffs and ancient mills line the river so not surprisingly the valley of the Célé is a little touristy. But thankfully only a little!

The minor road up the valley sees some traffic, but also a lot of families out cycling. The river is small and friendly with a gentle current and bubbling little rapids, almost all of it class 1. Water quality was poor when we visited the river in 2000 but has improved since then. You could imagine this river as being something out of 'Wind in the Willows' perhaps - there's certainly overhanging willow trees, and lots of fish to be seen in the green water.

Canoe Camping

This is an absolutely ideal choice for easy canoe camping - especially for a young family or beginners. There's a string of conveniently spaced, pleasant riverside campsites close to small picturesque villages. Several companies offer canoe hire, return transport, and will look after all the arrangements for you if you want. The minor road up the valley is smooth and level (perhaps an old railway line?) and follows the river closely so if you want to do your own shuttles by cycle or hitching then this should be easy. (Fluffy's Top Tip - take your roller blades for the shuttle!).

We suggest you make your first camp at Brengues and on the first day paddle down to here, then maybe another 3 days of gentle canoeing to finish in the river Lot at Bouzies - a grand climax to the trip.

Off the river

There's a surfeit of old villages nestling in the cliffs next to the river, waiting to be explored - along with old abbeys, priories, churches, castles, chateau's, mills, and caves. There's also some fine hikes to cliff top viewpoints and some pleasant bike rides along the valley. The local tourist offices have leaflets on walks and bike rides. We have to say that this is not a great centre for bungy-jumping, canyoning, paragliding, or ice climbing!

Food and drink

Most of the campsites have simple bars and restaurants and the villages have some excellent restaurants - popular so you do need to book ahead.

Camping

We liked the Municipal site at **Brengues**, which had good shade and pastoral views. It was busy but quiet and had a friendly ambience with canoeing families of different nationalities. There are no riverside campsites upstream from here, but downstream there are riverside campsites at St Sulpice, Marcillac, and Cabrerets.

Maps and Guides

IGN Top25 sheet 2238O covers the top stretch and sheet 2544O covers the bottom section from St Sulpice. IGN Top 100 sheet 65 covers this river and the lower Lot.

Tourist Offices -

Figeac, tel: 05 65 34 06 25 — www.quercy.net/figeac
Marcilhac, tel: 05 65 40 68 44
Cahors, tel: 05 65 53 26 30 — www.tourisme-lot.com

Canoe Hire

Bouzies, Safaraid, tel: 05 65 30 74 47 — www.canoe-dordogne.com, email: safaraid@aol.com

Anglanat, Nature & Loisirs, tel: 05 65 30 25 69

Orniac, les Amis du Célé, tel: 05 65 31 26 73 — www.amisducele.com, email: amis.du.cele@wanadoo.fr

Other rivers

The Célé flows into the lower Lot and it's possible to carry on down this river, but it's big and flat, and has many barrages - so very different in character and perhaps an anticlimax. It's probably better to head for one of the other rivers in this guide book - the Tarn, upper Lot, and Dordogne are only a couple of hours drive.

Grand Vabre

A quiet paddle at the campsite

Boussac to Brengues	14 km of class 1	★	❀❀	☺☺
Water quality - OK.	Temp. - warm. 5 cumecs?		Busy?	<50

It's possible to start paddling from Figeac, which would add another 11km but the river is shallow and the valley wide and less scenic above Boussac, so we recommend putting in here at the bridge, or 3 km downstream at Corn.

The river is shallow and occasional wading may be needed, but in essence this is a pleasant, safe, friendly, bimble with fine views as you enter the canyon part of the valley. We recommend a stop at **Espagnac** which is an incredibly pretty little village clustered around the remains of the 12th century Priory of Notre Dame (this is now converted into holiday gites). Fluffy was delighted to find a super little café at the back of the priory that sold home made ice cream.

As you approach **Brengues** there is the Camping *'le Moulin Vieux'* on the right hand site, with swimming pool and other up-market facilities and then after the bridge there is the much cheaper municipal campsite. A rough rock weir is just below the bridge and will probably need you to slide the boat over it. There is a good hotel/restaurant in the village and a fine little walk from here takes you up to *le Chateau des Anglais* - the ruins of a fortified house built high up into the cliff face with excellent views down the valley.

Grand Vabre

Brengues to Marcilhac | **10 km of class 1** | ★ | ❀❀ | ☺☺

Water quality - OK. | Temp. - warm. 5 cumecs? | Busy? <50

Here's another scenic stretch with the campsite and swimming pool at St Sulpice coming up after 6km, conveniently sited for a break. The village of **St Sulpice** is a little away from the river, with the houses built into the cliff face. All wonderfully picturesque and well worth exploring.

Two swooping big bends of the valley, framed by white limestone cliffs, brings you to **Marcilac** and the campsite upstream of the village. Highlight of the village is the old abbey and mill. A barrage here needs to be either portaged on the right or shot via a long sloping glissière on the left - this looks rather daunting but was quite harmless when we ran it - just a lovely little whoosh which I suppose should be given a class 2 rating. The village is a little touristy - we even saw a coach party! - and it has couple of restaurants, bars and shops.

Marcilhac to Cabrerets | **18 km of class 1 (2)** | ★★ | ❀❀ | ☺☺

Water quality - OK. | Temp. - warm. 5 cumecs? | Busy? <50

Scenery and the river continue much the same for 8km as far as **Sauliac** where you can see the caves and houses built into the cliffs where people used to live in the troubled times of the 100 years war. Apparently the less mobile used to be hauled up in great wicker work baskets. There is a picnic spot and launch site just upstream of the village and this is a popular starting point for hire canoes.

The next section, is probably the best for both scenery and paddling as the valley narrows into a more pronounced canyon and the river becomes more constrained as it goes bubbling over little bedrock rapids. The river cuts along the base of cliffs in places, very reminiscent of the Tarn or the Ardeche, and some of these rapids might possibly be an easy class 2-. After 3 km there is a canoe hire base at **Orniac** with the possibilities of refreshments and then another 3 km brings you to *'la Fontaine de la Pescalerie'* where a cave resurgent pours out of the cliff as a splendid green waterfall.

A couple of km brings you to the approaches to **Cabrerets** where there is a youth campsite on the left bank, and some dramatic looking swings bolted into the cliffs on the right cliff overhanging the river. The main public camp site is after the bridge. Set in a commanding position overlooking the river is the 14th century *Chateau Contaut-Biron,* whilst high on up on the cliff tops is the imposing *'Chateau du Diable'* - used as a base by the English from which to rape and pillage in the 100 years war.

A half hour walk above the town is one of France's top caves, **the 'Grottes de Pech Merle'** with its famous prehistoric cave paintings. This gets a *** rating in the Michelin Guide as a "must do" attraction. Unfortunately, we cannot comment on it as Fluffy doesn't like cold dark places, and instead our plebeian duck insisted on relaxing in the sunshine with a cold beer!

Cabrerets to Bouzies	**6 km of class 1 (2)**	★★	❁❁	☺☺
Water quality - OK.	Temp. - warm. 5 cumecs?			Busy? <50

The river continues in its tight gorge, sandwiched between the sweeping limestone cliffs and a highly photogenic view back upstream to the two Chateau Contaut-Biron. After 3km the little village of **Conduche** is on the right, the river bends under rail and road bridges and then the little world of the world of the Vallée du Célé is left behind as you paddle out onto the broad flat waters of the river Lot.

Look back upstream and you can see **St Cirque-Lapopie**, dubbed the 'prettiest village in France', perched on top of the cliffs in the distance. If you paddle over to the left hand bank, you will come to the lock island (the river Lot has been restored for navigation by pleasure cruisers) and just below the towpath is carved as an over-hanging ledge in the cliff face, decorated with a huge bas-relief carving by D..Monnier. This tow path was used in past centuries to haul the barges upstream, using horses or oxen on the easy stretches but with great teams of men wading through the water to haul the boats up the rapids. These teams of bargees had a fearsome reputation for toughness and debauched behaviour that has survived down the centuries - perhaps some of this has rubbed off in the certain wariness of landlubbers towards strange 'boat people'?

Another kilometre or two of flat water allows you to muse on such topics, or perhaps to go for a swim. **Bouzies** comes in sight after the railway bridge and the usual take out is on the left bank, and before the road bridge. There is a large public car park here, stepped back a 100m from the river, and several bars, restaurants and ice cream shops in the village.

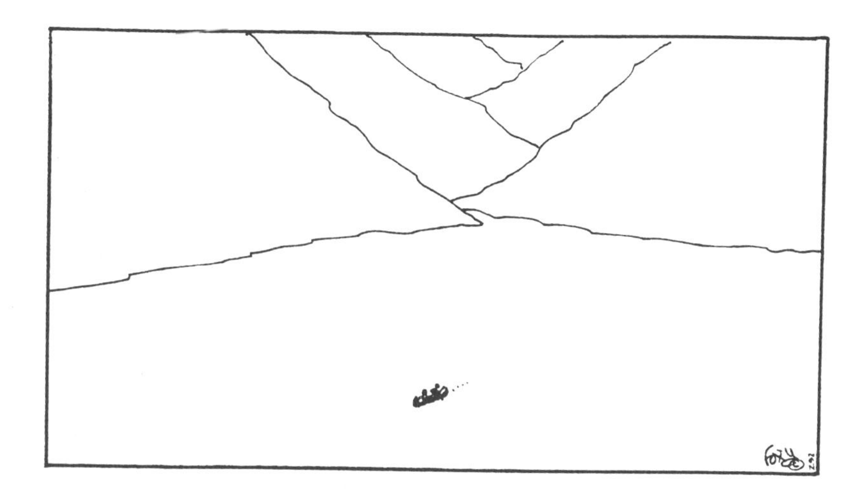

On the friendly confines of the tree-lined Célé Herbert
had managed to keep his agoraphobia under control,
but now they had reached the wide and mighty river Lot...

Célé - shooting the glissière at Marcilhac.

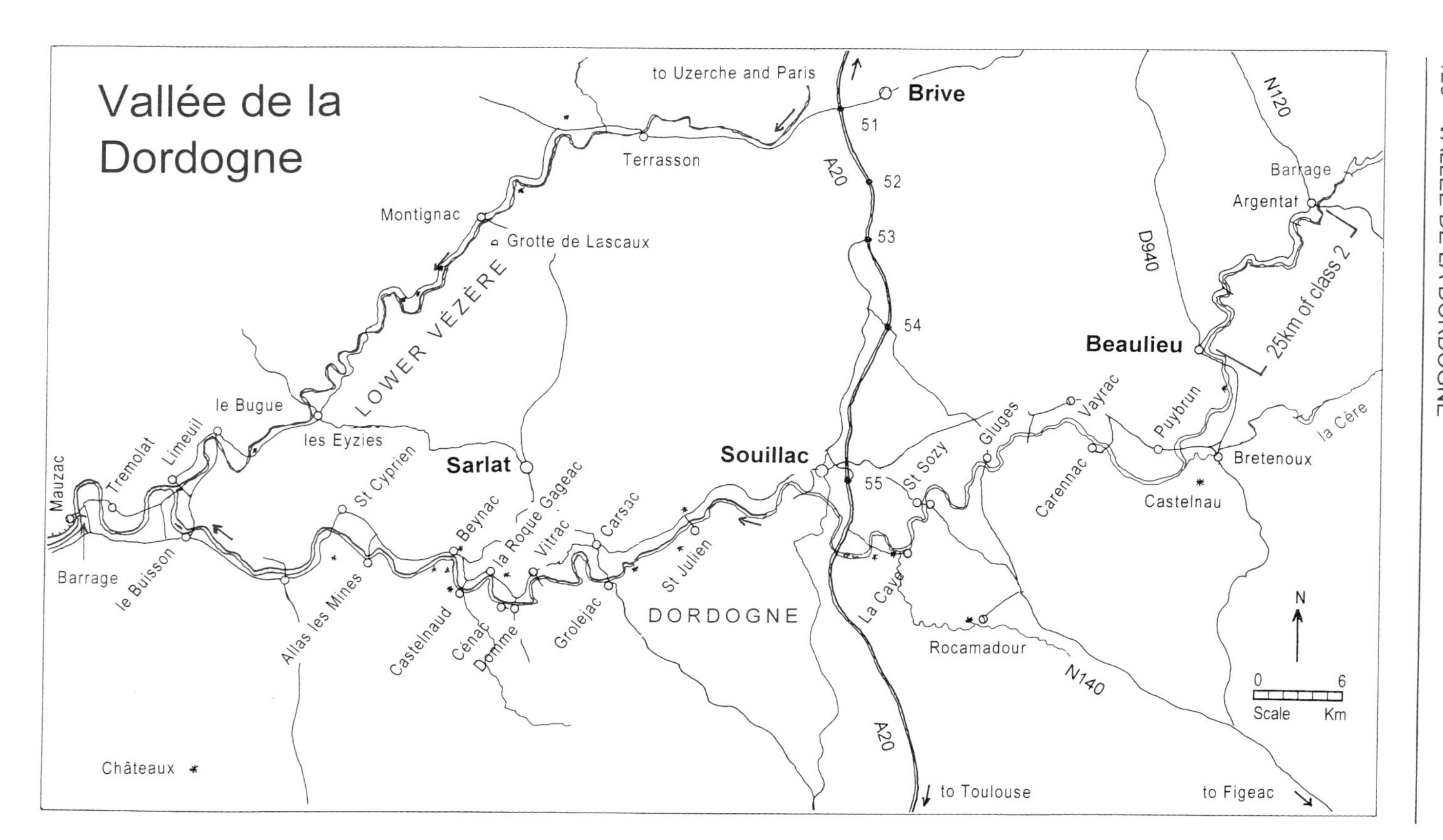
Vallée de la Dordogne
to Uzerche and Paris
Brive
51
52
53
54
55
A20
N120
Barrage
Argentat
D940
25km of class 2
Terrasson
Montignac
Grotte de Lascaux
LOWER VÉZÈRE
Beaulieu
Vayrac
Puybrun
la Cère
Bretenoux
Castelnau
Gluges
St Sozy
Carennac
le Bugue
les Eyzies
Limeuil
Tremolat
Mauzac
Sarlat
Souillac
St Cyprien
Beynac
la Roque Gageac
Vitrac
Carsac
St Julien
Barrage
le Buisson
Allas les Mines
Castelnaud
Cénac
Domme
Grolejac
DORDOGNE
La Cave
Rocamadour
N140
N
0
6
Scale
Km
Châteaux
A20
to Toulouse
to Figeac

Dordogne

Summary

Run	Class	Km	Stars	Scen.	Fluffy	Busy	Notes
Argentat to Beaulieu	2(2+)	25	★★	❁❁	☺	<50	Fast wide river, a sporty run.
Beaulieu to Souillac	1 (2)	55	★★	❁❁	☺☺	<200	A Classic canoe touring stretch.
Souillac to Beynac	1	44	★	❁❁	☺☺	≥200	Famous villages, popular tourist run
Beynac to Mauzac	1	44	★	❁	☺	<50	Quiet, mellow run.

The Dordogne is one of the grand rivers of France, in a valley famous for its scenery, historic towns, villages, chateaux, and gastronomic delights. The vast majority of these sights are just a stone's throw from the river, so a canoe trip is a perfect way to explore the valley - couple this with a clean, transparent green river, bubbling class 1 and 2 rapids, no portages (well almost), plentiful campsites, and great scenery and you can see why this is one of the canoe touring classics in the world.

The River

The Dordogne rises high in the Massif Central near Mont Dore, but most of the upper reaches, the Gorges de la Dordogne are now submerged by a series of hydro dams and reservoirs, so the river is now only navigable from Argentat. This middle section down to Beaulieu is a fine stretch with the best white water and assured water levels though-out the summer - also relatively un-crowded. Below here, as you go down the river towards Sarlat you travel into the most famous part of the Dordogne valley, and the river gets busier, day by day, with lots of tourists in the summer.

The river is a popular half day canoe trip and we are told that there may be as many as 2000 people a day on the stretch from la Domme to Beynac. However, this is an exceptional day and even in the height of summer you won't see anything like this number. This is a large wide river, something comparable to the Thames (but a lot cleaner) so there is plenty of room for lots of canoes - however, if you have the choice, then we recommend that you come here off season or avoid this most popular stretch. Further upstream the river has less tourists, and in our opinion has better paddling and scenery!

So which are the best sections? Well, as noted, Beaulieu to Argentat has the best white water. If you have four days then Beaulieu to Souillac is probably the best section for canoe or kayak touring. If you only have a day then the 18km from Gluges to Pinsac is probably the most scenic stretch. Note that all the canoe hire companies run shuttle bus services back up the valley, and provided they have room, which they normally do, they will be happy to sell any paddler a bus seat back to your starting point for a nominal charge. Canoeing is regulated and limited to the hours of 0900 to 1800 so that the fishermen can enjoy a quiet morning or evening - this is a clean, clear, green river and you will be amazed how many fish you can see.

Canoe Camping

This is one of the most popular rivers in Europe for canoe camping with 157 km of free-flowing, unspoilt river and almost no portages and is typically done as a relaxed 10 day trip. Alternatively if you want a shorter trip then Argentat to Souillac makes a fine 5 day trip.

A few canoe hire companies specialise in multi-day trips where they will hire you the canoes, waterproof barrels for your gear, paddles, etc: book your campsites for you if you wish, and then transport you back to the start and your car from where-ever you end up - all at such incredibly good value (an Old Town 17ft canoe cost us 50 Euros for 4 days) that many paddlers prefer to hire rather than have the hassle of transporting canoes from their home country.

If you have a choice then do try and plan your trip to avoid the summer peak season so that you miss the crowds. We ignored this advice and deliberately researched this river in early August, and found it less busy than we had expected and still an immensely enjoyable experience. We didn't book our campsites ahead and although most looked full, all had a site or two free - even if technically full, we suspect that if you arrive by river, they will find you a spot to pitch a tent overnight.

Off the river

The valley of the Dordogne is famous for its beautifully preserved historic towns and villages. All the way down the river are splendid châteaux perched on cliffs - these cry out to be explored. This is a main tourist area so there are many other things to do, with evening concerts, village fetes, fireworks, and markets - it's always worth popping in to the local tourist office to find out details of any special events. Your campsite will also probably have a rack over-flowing with promotional leaflets for other ideas!

This is probably not a great area for mountain biking as the roads are busy in the summer months, but this is less true as you go up the valley, and the area around Argentat has several good routes.

Food and drink

The Périgord region is famous for its gastronomic specialities, particularly foie gras, and though-out the Dordogne valley there is a wide choice of restaurants and cafes. This is a main tourist area, so we cynically expected that everywhere would be pizza and chips, or hyped up, over-priced menus, and yes there are these establishments, but we looked a little further and were pleasantly surprised and had some good meals out at reasonable prices. We have made a few recommendations in the descriptions below.

Camping

There are numerous riverside campsites all the way down the Dordogne, so this makes it perfect for canoe-camping. Tourist offices and websites will give you a full list. Note that you would be wise to book ahead on the popular sites - you can email or fax the campsite for a plan of the site and select an individual site if this is important to you. Arrive on spec and you may well get the pitch next to the toilet block, or 500m from the river! It's almost unfair to recommend individual campsites when there is such a selection, but here are a few to get you started:

ɪrdogne - Beaulieu, 12th Century chapel of St Pierre. Sue Richardson

ɪrdogne - 'le Battut' rapid upstream of Beaulieu.

Dordogne - Suzy below St Sozy.

rdogne - family canoeing at Montford.

orges de la Vézère - below Vigeois.

Sue Richardson

Beaulieu - 5km upstream from the town is *'Camping la Berge Ombragée'* - tel: 05 55 91 01 17, email: berge.ombragee@freesbee.fr. This was one of our favourite sites. It's a small friendly quiet site 'camping au naturelle' in a grassy orchard on the banks of the river. Your pitch is a walnut tree! Hot showers of course, and a small bar. In the town of Beaulieu, *'Camping des Isles'* - tel: 05 55 91 02 65, is a larger 3 star site with good facilities and very helpful owner.

At **St Sozy,** *'Camping les Borgnes'* - tel, 05 65 32 21 48 is a shady site with a huge swimming pool, bar, and good value restaurant. When we were there this site was pleasantly un-crowded and good value.

Maps and Guides

IGN Top 100 sheet 48 covers the whole of the Dordogne and the Vézère so is a best buy if you are paddling in this area.

There is an FFCK 'Dordogne 'Guide de Rivière' which is worth buying if you are planning a long cruise. Our edition is 1990, but hopefully it will now have been updated - available from 'le Canotier' and main tourist offices. An alternative is the more up-to-date, locally published guide, called 'Rivière Dordogne - Carte-Guide de la Déscente' which is available from local book shops.

The Michelin Green guide to Dordogne, Berry and Limousin has excellent sections on the Dordogne valley. "The Dordogne" by Stephen Brook (an appropriate name!) published by George Philip, covers the history and current status of the region very well and is beautifully illustrated with photos.

Tourist Offices -

Argentat, tel: 05 55 28 16 05	www.cg19.fr
Beaulieu, tel: 05 55 91 09 94	
Souillac, tel: 05 65 37 81 56	www.souillac.com
Sarlat, tel: 05 55 29 98 78	www.sarlat-tourisme.com

Canoe Hire

There are numerous local companies offering day and half day trips - please contact the local tourist office for a list. Note that there is a wide choice of canoes, kayaks, and sit-on-tops with some quality boats available if you ask for them.

Several companies specialise in multi-day trips with a daily return shuttle bus service running back up the valley - two of the main ones are:

Oxygène ADPA (Safaraid),	www.adpa.net,
tel: 05 55 28 86 45.	(recommended)
Saga-team, tel: 05 55 28 84 84	

Other rivers

We recommend the Gorges de Vézère and upper Vézère, which are about an hour's drive away and offer two fine day runs that are pleasantly different in character from the Dordogne. The lower Vézère, Lot and Célé are also relatively close and well worth considering.

One hundred kilometres upstream, above the dams and reservoirs, the upper Dordogne is just a small mountain river that has a 16 km section of class 3-4. between St Sauves and Chalameyroux. This normally only has sufficient water in the spring and autumn.

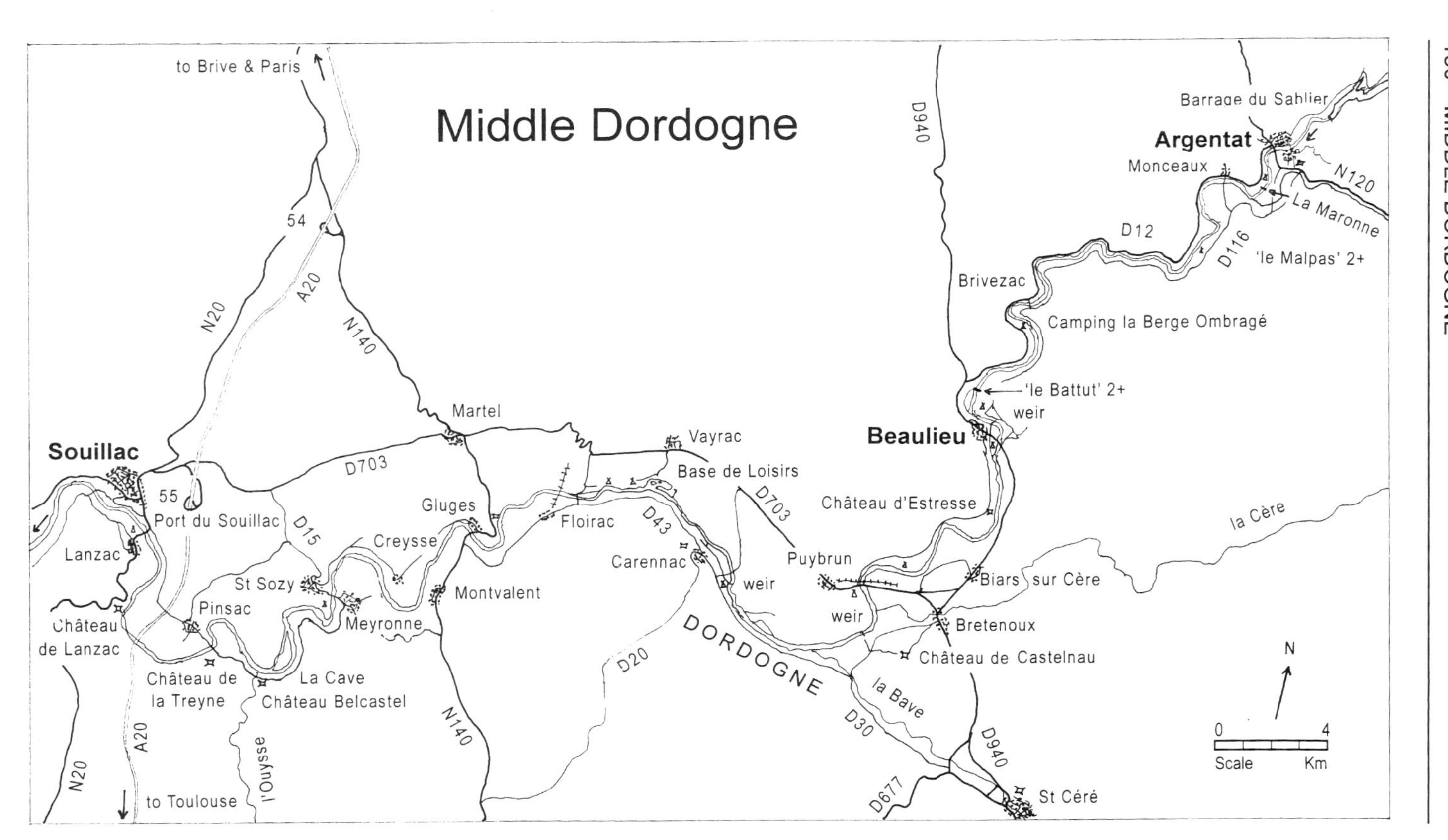
Middle Dordogne
to Brive & Paris
54
N20
A20
N140
Martel
D703
Souillac
55
Port du Souillac
D15
Lanzac
Château
de Lanzac
Pinsac
St Sozy
Creysse
Gluges
Meyronne
Montvalent
Château de
la Treyne
La Cave
Château Belcastel
N140
A20
N20
to Toulouse
l'Ouysse
Floirac
Vayrac
Base de Loisirs
D703
D43
Carennac
weir
D20
DORDOGNE
Puybrun
weir
Château d'Estresse
Beaulieu
'le Battut' 2+
weir
Brivezac
Camping la Berge Ombragé
D940
D12
D116
'le Malpas' 2+
Argentat
Monceaux
Barrage du Sablier
N120
La Maronne
la Cère
Biars
sur Cère
Bretenoux
Château de Castelnau
la Bave
D30
D940
D677
St Céré
N
0
4
Scale
Km

Argentat to Beaulieu	**25 km of class 2 (2+)**	★★	❀❀	☺
Water quality - good.	Temp. - cool. 20 cumecs?		Busy?	<50

Summary

Argentat to Monceaux 4km, Brivezac 13km, Beaulieu 8km.

The Dordogne here is quite a big river - something comparable to the Spey or the Tay in Scotland, with a fast current and some chunky class 2 rapids to add interest to what is otherwise mainly a class 1 run. The scenery is pleasantly pastoral with green pastures, orchards and woodland lining the hillsides each side of the river. Argentat and Beaulieu are both historic riverside trading towns, with well preserved picturesque quay sides. There are no major hazards and usually no portages are needed so this makes it a really great run for the canoeist with a little experience. Note that you are required to wear buoyancy aids on this section.

Description

At **Argentat** we suggest that you **put in** at the ancient quay side on the river right upstream of the old bridge - when we were here they were building a reproduction of one of the 'gabariers', the old wooden boats that used to trade on the river. The centre of the town, shops and tourist office, are all only 5 minutes walk away. From the old bridge there is a great view of the quayside, the medieval houses (with their quaint pepper-pot turrets), and perhaps your canoe spoiling the photo in the foreground?

There is a water gauge on the left above the bridge, low water is usually reckoned to be 50 to 90cm and medium water 90cm to 1.50m. 50 cm on the gauge is about 11 cumecs, 90cm = 32 cumecs and 1.50m is 100 cumecs.

There are several campsites and canoe hire bases on the right bank in the next 2 km and then look out for the first big rapid **'le Malpas'**, normally marked in high season by camera vultures perched on the rocks on the right. You can avoid their attentions by taking the easier route going left of the small island - however the right hand route is testing and more fun!

The *Maronne* river comes in on the left below and then a km further is the road bridge leading to the village of **Monceaux**. There's a landing spot 100m down stream on the right for ice creams.

The river continues with a fine current that whooshes you along at 2-3km an hour, running over shingle and boulders, with many beds of crowsfeet and water buttercups. Look down into the transparent green water and you will see countless fish. The rapids are all obvious with straight-forward lines and wave trains with a few eddies and scope for attempts at surfing.

Brivezac bridge is about 17km below Argentat. There is a landing, cafe and a small 'camping naturelle' site on the left, however little shade, so we recommend continuing on another 2km where *'Camping la Berge Ombragée'* is on the right bank, and offers a friendly little bar and delightful campsite. Two km downstream look out for **'le Battut'**, an entertaining class 2+ rapid formed by an old stone weir - this has some big waves that can swamp an open canoe and then the current carries you into rocks and trees on the left bank where the wet sleeping bag gremlins await.....

Another kilometre and the town of **Beaulieu** comes into sight around the bend. We recommend **taking out** on the right bank to and explore the town. Beaulieu has a wealth of delightful medieval houses lining a maze of narrow streets and the famous 12th century Romanesque church of St-Pierre. Despite being so attractive, it's pleasantly un-crowded and seemingly few tourists. On the waterfront there is another 12th century chapel in a particularly beautiful setting and this is now a local history museum. We had a fine meal in yet another 12th century building, the *Hotel le Turenne*.

There is a municipal campsite upstream of the town on the left bank, or the 3 star *'Camping des Iles'* which is on an island (below the barrage) reached from the right bank, and thus more convenient for the centre of the town. **Beware of the barrage** that runs across the full width of the river and is unshootable. To continue down the river, land on the left bank by the canoe base building and either portage, or scout and shoot the small, but amusing, glissière that follows.

To go to 'Camping des Iles', either take the glissière (which runs to the left of an island necessitating a short upstream paddle at the end of the island to get to the campsite on the right bank of the river) or land to the right of the barrage and portage across a small bridge into the top of the campsite.

Dordogne above Beaulieu - 'le Battut' rapid.

Beaulieu to Souillac	**55 km of class 1 (2)**	★★	❁❁	☺☺
Water quality - good.	Temp. - cool. 20 cumecs?		Busy? <200	

Summary

Beauliu to Puybrun 11km, Vayrac 13km, St Sozy 16km, Souillac 15km

This is the classic stretch for canoe-camping, with the scenery getting better and better as you go down the river. Lots of historic villages, chateaux, and interest off the river, coupled with lots of mainly easy class 1 rapids and a fair current to push you along. Justly popular with the knowledgeable canoe tourist, there aren't too many day hires on this section - only in the last 15km from St Sozy does it start getting really busy.

Description

At **Beaulieu** you can either start upstream of the barrage - see preceding section - or put in below, either at the Camping des Isles (if you are staying here), or on the left bank about 200m upstream of the bridge. The river threads its way through some small islands and the bridge, with some bubbling little class 1 rapids, then after a km surprise, surprise there is another big class 2 rapid with some nice waves for surfing.

Below here, the river is flat for a couple of km until the main road is alongside on the left. Then it settles into a pattern of an easy class 1 rapid every km, normally a straight forward bimble down between gravel bars and a small wave train. There is a handy embarkation point at the small village of la Serre on the left and then 500m below on the right is *'Camping du Pont'* another pleasant campsite. A further km brings you to the main road bridge at **Puybrun**.

Looming up ahead on the skyline is the great medieval fortress of **Castelnau-Bretenoux**, particularly impressive at sunset with the sandstone ramparts glowing a fiery red against a blue sky. The Cère river joins from the left after a km and below here look out for an old weir which can normally be shot on the right or slide over left (to be different, you could always start your trip 4 km up the Cère at *'Camping La Bourgnatell'* in Bretenoux). This is the most convenient spot to visit Castelnau which is 2 km walk. Continuing on, the river gently curves to the right and the valley sides on the left build up, until you can see the village of Carennac on the skyline in the distance.

Before you reach the village, you come to a weir with a mill stream off to the left and *'Camping l'Eaux Vives'* (noisy on the one occasion we stayed here). Keep left and paddle down this old mill stream for a km or so, under the road bridge, to come out on the old quay at the foot of Carennac village (if you don't want to visit the village, then shoot the glissière and carry on down the main river).

Carennac is one of the most picturesque villages in the Dordogne valley noted for its pretty little medieval houses, incredibly convoluted roof lines, fascinating towers, quaint little turrets - all on an impressive hill top location over-looking the river, so well worth a little wander and perhaps an ice cream?

The Dordogne has, over the centuries, moved away from the old quay so to rejoin the main river you need to paddle across to where you can see a little gap in the trees and a wooden plank footbridge. There's a shallow stone shoot here, which takes the water back to the main river. Land on the left to inspect - the slide has a chain across to discourage you from shooting it - and it does look a bit of a rough, so the sensible alternative is to take the short portage path.

Continuing on, the river keeps up its pace with some class 1 rapids in the next 2km, and then on the right is the *Base de Loisirs* and large well-equipped campsite near **Vayrac.** On the left bank is a vista of sweeping limestone cliffs, rolling green hills, and cute little houses poking up through the trees.

You pass a road and rail bridge and then the imposing Chateau de Mirandol comes into view on top of the cliffs ahead. The river flows right underneath the Chateau with over-hanging cliffs rising straight out of the current. This sweeps you around the right bend and into more over-hanging cliffs now on the left. This is all exciting scenery and fun paddling, but take care on these bends as the current carries you into the cliffs in what the French call a '*drossage*'.

Gluges bridge comes into sight, and there are canoe hire bases, and a campsite on the right as you go round the corner. There is public access and a picnic site on a nice grassy area below the bridge on the left - also another campsite downstream. The river bends left again under the ochre coloured cliffs and then there is another '*drossage*' rapid on the right. The river then quietens a little in a long straight - time to look around and count the birds - we saw buzzards, kingfishers, swallows, dippers, and herons and egrets on this stretch.

The river curves round to the right in an attractively wild setting, with cliffs, little beaches, and smooth sculptured rock ledges for swimming from - a great place for a picnic lunch (or wild camping - if this were allowed). Another km brings you to people again with a public access right for the pretty little village of **Creysse** (hidden though the trees) and campsites on both banks.

Three kilometres around this long, long bend brings you to the road bridge. **Meyronne** is left - a small picturesque village with an excellent gastronomic hotel/restaurant and a crowded '*Camping du Plage*' below the bridge. On the right bank is the village of **St Sozy,** less picturesque and a kilometre from the river. Next to the river on the right bank and upstream of the bridge is the small spacious '*Village de Vacances du Port*' (tel: 5 65 32 21 78), and then below the bridge, right is '*Camping les Borgnes*' which we rated as spacious, friendly, and good value.

Pleasant paddling continues with a wide river and a good current carrying you along for the next 3 km and then up ahead appear the high cliffs of the '*Roch de Monges*' which drop an impressive 200m straight to the river. There is another campsite on the left bank below here. In the distance ahead are more impressive cliffs on the left, surmounted by the magnificent *Chateau le Belcastel.* The river sweeps along the base of these cliffs, but proceed cautiously and look out for a cave resurgent which you can paddle into. This is the exit where the underground stream comes out of the **Grottes de Lacave** and this cave makes an exciting expedition if you have remembered to keep your head torches handy (even more exciting if you haven't!). You can actually paddle up some 20m into the cave, but probably the best thing is to tie up your boat to the old rusty iron mooring ring at the entrance, and then wade up the stream. Beware the Trolls, Orcs and ice cold water !

The little village of **La Cave** is about 500m down on the left at the confluence of the narrow canyon of the Ouysse (GR6 footpath runs along the bottom of this and looks like another interesting expedition).

Carrying on around the long bend on the right are more cliffs dropping to river level with caves and dark holes that beckon any deviant canoeist who has now acquired troglodyte tendencies. All this fun ends at **Pinsac** bridge where there are canoe hire bases, campsite, and ice creams.

Fluffy was very relieved to be out of these dark, damp holes and enjoyed the next 5km - just drifting along a nice wide river and soaking up the sunshine and the scenery. The valley is wider and more pastoral, with green rolling valley sides. The A20 autoroute swoops over the valley from hill to hill on a high elegant viaduct, and a kilometre below perched on another cliff top is yet another Chateau (the Chateau de Lanzac) and from here it's a mellow scenic km paddle round a long bend, more cliffs on the right, beaches and bathers left, to the main road bridge at the Port du **Souillac**. The main campsite and egress is downstream of the bridge on the left, with a handy bar and café at the entrance. Souillac is a town with a tourist sparkle of life, a good range of traditional local shops to replenish the icebox and a typical French market held on Fridays.

Lower Dordogne - downstream from the battlements of la Domme. *Dave Hallewell*

Souillac to Beynac	**44 km of class 1**	★	❁❁	☺☺
Water quality - OK.	Temp. - warm 25 cumecs?		Busy? >200	

Summary

Souillac to St Julien 12km, Grolejac 8km, Cenac 14km, Beynac 10km.

This is **the classic stretch** of the Dordogne and a great trip. If you go in the middle of summer then you do have to have to appreciate that whilst not quite bank to bank plastic, there will be a lot of other boats as this is the most popular stretch of the river for hire canoes - it's an easy, wide river, still with a good current, class one riffles, and no significant hazards or dangers. The scenery is splendid as the river cuts huge loops between impressive swoops of limestone cliffs, surmounted by famous villages and chateaux. There are many beaches and riverside campsites every couple of kilometres, with their fleets of plastic canoes drawn up on the beach, so we have limited our description to the main public access points.

Description

There is a public put-in on at the camp site on the left bank below the bridge at **Port du Souillac** and then after 2 km another access below the next bridge at Cieurac. Access at St Julien de Lampon is again on the left downstream of the bridge. At **Groléjac** public access is again on the left bank below the second bridge. A kilometre below here the current sweeps you into the cliffs on the left, so beginners should stay right. This is the start of the famous Cingle de Montford as the river cuts a huge loop. The little village of **Montford** is on the right with the Castle perched above the river just downstream - named after Simon de Montford who siezed it in 1214. It was then, over the centuries, destroyed and rebuilt no less than four times. There's a good riverside campsite, *'Camping La Bouysse'*, 1.5km downstream on the big right hand bend with high cliffs towering opposite.

The next public access is 3km later at **Vitrac**, again on the left bank downstream of the bridge. Downstream from here, you come round the bend and there ahead high on top of the crags is the fortified village of **Domme**, one of the most impressive and famous sites on the river. This is well worth a visit some time during your stay. The public embarkation point is the beach on the left below **Cenac** bridge.

Continuing on the river another 4km brings you to **La Roque Gageac** where the quaint little houses nestle into the cliffs with the river quay side in front. All rather marred by the main road between river and village - so best viewed from the far bank with the late afternoon sun colouring the houses a pretty gold hue.

There are another two campsites in the next 2km to the bridge at Castelnaud with a public landing above the bridge on the left. **Castelnaud** is a fine example of a medieval fortress and is well worth a visit. The Dordogne here formed the front line in the Hundred years war between English and French forces - there is a great view from the ramparts and you can see the fierce rival castle of Beynac, 3km away on the other side of the river.

There are two riverside campsites on the right before you reach **Beynac** where there is a public landing below the village on the right. A steep lane winds up through the picturesque medieval houses to this mighty fortress which was captured by Richard the Lion Heart. Another impressive castle, splendid panorama, and it's difficult to say which of the two rivals most deserves a visit!

Beynac to Mauzac	**44 km of class 1**	★	❉	☺
Water quality - OK.	Temp. - warm. 25 cumecs?		Busy?	<50

Summary

Beynac to Siorac 17km, Limeuil 14km, Mauzac 13km.

Still good scenery, however there are no longer any really famous tourist sites so this section is less popular for canoe hire and you will find this much quieter than the stretch above Beynac. The river is also quieter in the other sense with a slower current, wide, and almost no rapids, so this makes for less fun canoeing. A hydro barrage at Muazac dams the river and makes the last few km a slog so many people finish at Limeuil at the confluence with the Vézère. There are fewer riverside campsites on this stretch so we have tried to note these below.

Description

There is a public access point just downstream of **Beynac** on the right bank, and then landing points on the left bank at the little villages of les Milandes after 3km, Envaux, another 2km, and above the bridge at **Allas les Mines.** The first riverside campsite is another 2km on the right, just above the village of **St Cyprien**. There is a public landing here, immediately below the first bridge on the left bank. After here it's 6km to the next campsite at **Siorac**, on the left downstream of the bridge.

Le Buisson, a further 9km, is a larger village with a campsite and public landing on the left upstream of the bridge. 4km then brings you to the confluence with the **Vézère**, its two bridges, and the old port of **Limeuil**. This thankfully doesn't attract hordes of tourists, but is just a fine old village, which is an interesting and enjoyable place to explore. '*Camping Le Port de Limeuil*' is on the left after the confluence and has been recommended by many paddlers.

The Dordogne now makes two huge sinuous loops first to the right and then to the left, the second one is the '*Cingle de Trémolat*' with the village of **Trémolat** (and campsite) on the right below the two bridges. This is another pretty little village that deserves an explore - particularly interesting is the 12th century church which is a fine example of a fortified Romanesque church. From here it's just 4km round the bend to village of **Mauzac**. There is a campsite on the right above the village, or alternatively land in the village on the right underneath the rail bridge.

The barrage is highly dangerous and if you wish to continue down river you need to take the old canal off to the right and then portage 100m down to the approved mini harbour launch point. At Bergerac take out right at the slipway and large cobbled parking area.

Purists will of course wish to continue another 130km to the sea, but this is now a large river, navigable by tug boats and barges - Fluffy doesn't like rivers of this type so this lower river is outside the scope of this book.

Cormorant

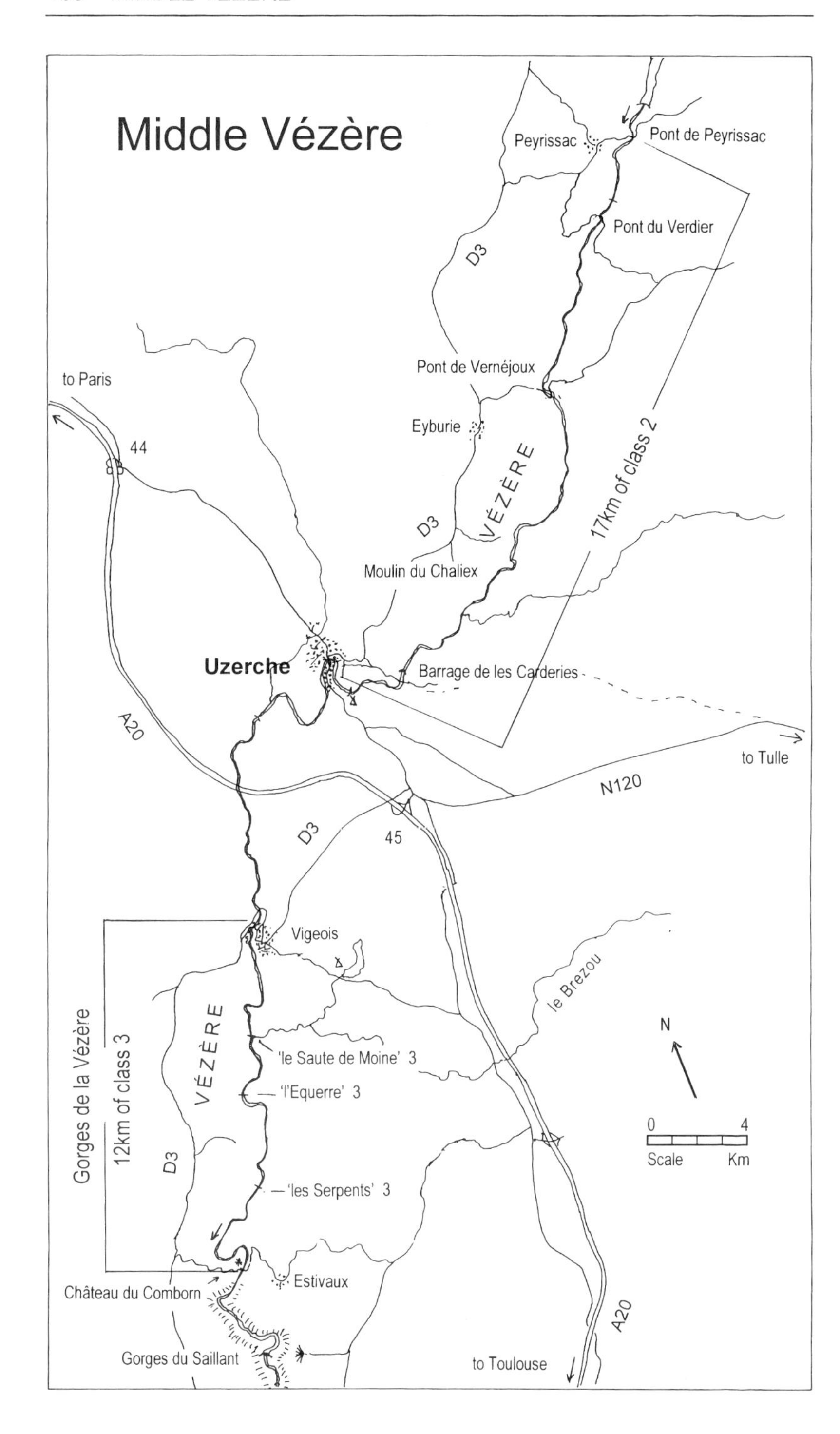

Middle Vézère
Peyrissac
Pont de Peyrissac
Pont du Verdier
D3
Pont de Vernéjoux
Eyburie
VÉZÈRE
17km of class 2
D3
Moulin du Chaliex
to Paris
44
Uzerche
Barrage de les Carderies
A20
to Tulle
N120
D3
45
Vigeois
le Brezou
N
VÉZÈRE
'le Saute de Moine' 3
'l'Equerre' 3
Gorges de la Vézère
12km of class 3
0
4
Scale
Km
D3
'les Serpents' 3
Estivaux
Château du Comborn
Gorges du Saillant
to Toulouse
A20

Vézère

Summary

River and run	Class	Km	Stars	Scen.	Fluffy	Busy	Notes
Peyrissac to Uzerche	2	17	★★	❁❁	☺	<10	Delightful, small, unspoilt river.
Vigeois to Estivaux	3	12	★★★	❁❁	-	<10	Granite gorge - a fun kayak run.
Montignac to Limeuil	1	47	★	❁❁	☺	<200	Famous pre-historic caves.

The River

The Vézère rises on a big green area in the N.W. of the Massif Central called the Millevaches plateau. The upper river twists through granite hills and is more reminiscent of a Scottish river, but then in its lower reaches, just before it joins the Dordogne, it becomes more typical of the Massif Central as it cuts its way through a limestone plateau. Our description is mainly of the upper river and the Gorges de Vézère, because we think these offer such good paddling. .

The old town of Uzerche, and the top two sections are only ten minutes off the A20 autoroute from Paris to Toulouse so this makes a great stop-over and warm up river for any kayaker headed for the Pyrenees or Spain. It's almost undiscovered by the paddling fraternity, and there is little canoe tourism so this is just a great river to build into your itinerary - different to the rivers of the southern Massif Central - not as scenic perhaps, but with some great paddling and an interesting area.

The river is dam controlled and there is usually a daily release on most days throughout the summer - but **check this before paddling**. at the canoe base in Uzerche

Further upstream at Treignac there is a fine 11km section of class 3-4, used for the World down river championships in year 2000 (more exactly, it's 3km of class 3, then 5km of class 4, then 3km of class 3). This rarely has sufficient water in high summer, but there is normally an organised release for the Whitsun weekend each year.

Canoe Camping

The upper sections described here don't lend themselves to canoe camping, but the lower Vézère from Montignac to Limeuil offers a scenic 3 day paddle with several riverside campsites and lots of pre-historic sites to visit.

Off the river

Uzerche is a fine sleepy old medieval town built on a hill surrounded by a bend of the river, largely by-passed by most tourists - so just a great place for leisurely exploration. For the really lazy there is a 'toy train' that takes you up, down and around this hillside town for a very reasonable 1.5 euros. For the more active there is a cycle route on an old railway line for some 20km east through fields and woods to the village of Seilhac.

Food and drink

Uzerche, offers several restaurants with good food and great value - our best buy was 8 euros for a traditional French 3 course meal! Local paddlers recommend 'Champraux Denise' on rue Porte Barachaude and the 'Auberge de la Vézère' at le Pont de Vernjoux - noted for its fresh fish and sweet chestnut ice cream. Fluffy recommends the home made chocolates from the Chocolatiere half way up the main hill in Uzerche.

Camping

Top recommendation has to be the municipal campsite in **Uzerche**, in a glorious riverside setting nestling below the old town. A superb location at the take-out for the upper Vézère, next to the Canoe Base, good facilities, great value, and the town is only five minutes walk. *Camping Municipal*, tel: 05 55 73 12 75. (Note, especially if you are here early season, that this site has camping huts available for rent). If this is full there are two sites at Vigeois, but these are not very convenient for the river. Note that there is a riverside Gite d'etape at the put-in at Vigeois - ideal for groups, tel: 05 55 98 90 86.

On the lower Vézère there are several riverside sites - details from the local tourist offices.

Maps and Guides

IGN Top 100 sheet 48 covers the whole of the Vézère and the Dordogne at a scale or 1:100,000 so is a best buy if you are paddling in this area.

The Conseil Regional de Limousin publish a free 64 page rivers guide 'Canoe-kayak en Limousin' that is available from main tourist offices, canoe bases, and le Canotier. This is especially useful if you are interested in paddling some of the smaller rivers early season.

The Canoe Base in Uzerche, the 'Base de la Minoterie' has an excellent webbsite: http://perso.wanadoo.fr/vezere.passion/

Tourist Offices

Uzerche, tel: 05 55 73 15 71
Montignac, tel: 05 53 51 82 60
les Eyzies, tel: 05 53 06 97 05
Tulle, tel: 05 55 29 98 78

Canoe Hire and rafting

For the upper Vézere and Gorges de la Vézère we recommend *the Base de la Minoterie* in Uzerche - a friendly, FFCK approved centre and next to the campsite. Tel: 05 55 73 02 84, email vezere.passion@wanadoo.fr.

For the lower Vézère there are numerous canoe hire companies - please ask the tourist offices above for an up to date list.

If water levels are sufficient then the Gorges de la Vézère make a great raft run, details from the Base de la Minoterie.

Other rivers

The upper Dordogne at Argentat is only about an hour's drive away so could be done as a day trip from Uzerche. The Corrèze may be worth a paddle if you are here early season - consult the Kayak Club in Tulle for local advice, tel: 05 55 26 64 15.

Peyrissac to Uzerche -	**17 km of class 2**	★★	❁❁	☺
Water quality - good.	Temp. - cool. 8 cumecs?		Busy? <10	

Summary
A very pleasant run, through completely unspoilt woodland and pastures, a bubbling clear current flowing over a golden sand bottom, mainly class 1, with granite boulders creating a few class 2 rapids - ideal for open canoes and conveniently finishing at the canoe base and campsite in Uzerche. Fluffy thought this was a great run, friendly and fun!

Description
Put in at **Peyrissac bridge**, in a pleasant, tranquil setting, just over the road from a laid-back café and bar. A good current and a few little rapids brings you after 2km to the old Moulin du Verdier - a sloping stone weir will probably need you to get out and slide your boat over it on the left.

Bedrock ledges and granite boulders, form a few little rapids, with the only real hazard being the occasional over-hanging beech, oak or chestnut tree (why we only gave it one Fluffy star). This stretch reminded us of an easy stretch of the River Dart in England with the same clear brown water smelling slightly of peat, and dappled sunlight gleams off the golden brown sand. Green moss, golden sand, grey granite stones, and water weed, create a kaleidoscope pattern of golds, bronzes and green. Open woodland alternates with the occasional cow pasture, kingfishers and dragon flies dart across the river, and a heron escorts you warily downstream. All very pleasant and nothing exciting or spectacular, but a bubbling current and only a couple of flat stretches.

The **Pont de Vernéjoux** is 7km from Peyrissac and there is access here on the right bank and the 'Auberge de la Vézère offers refreshment. About 2 km downstream, a fine old building on the left through the trees marks a bouncy little class 2 rapid at the confluence of a small stream, then after another km there is another old mill with a weir upstream - a class 2+ shoot right or a slide/portage on the left.

The river eases a bit, just a class 1 bimble with a helpful current for a couple of km and then the valley narrows, the sides become steeper with dense beech woods, and the river livens up as it makes a couple of tight bends. There's about four or so class 2 rapids in this section with little shoots over ledges and a few boulders to avoid - nothing difficult or scary, just friendly and fun. Through the trees on the right bank you can see the old mill at Chaleix, about 7km after Pont de Vernéjoux.

The river then eases off in the lead up to the **weir at les Carderies**. This is about a metre high - if the water is low then land on the extreme right to slide your boat over it - if the water is high then portage on the left. This is followed almost immediately by the old railway bridge which is high above the river, and again the river goes flat in the last km as it approaches the weir at the canoe base 'la Minoterie', the recommended take out, and the campsite. There is a superb glissière over the weir here that will definitely get you wet!

*The 9km from **Uzerche to Vigeois** can be paddled but is not recommended because it is mainly flat and requires two portages around dams.*

Vigeois to Estivaux	**12 km of class 3**	★★★ ❁❁	-
Water quality - good.	Temp. - cool. 15 cumecs?		Busy? <10

Summary

These **'Gorges de la Vézère'** are a superb kayak run, described by different paddlers as "entertaining", "lots of interest, but in no way scary", "feisty and fun". It makes a great run for rusty kayakers looking for a technical but easy warm up. Although not that hard, the river, and the rapids are very rocky, so it would be a technical rock dodge for open canoes and Fluffy was quite glad he gave it a miss - particularly as there was no ice cream shop at the take-out. Again, because the rapids are rocky and long, it would be a bumpy rough swim for any swimmers. So the good news is that this beautiful river is just that bit too difficult for beginners so there is little canoe hire, and on most days you will probably have the river to yourself.

The river has cut a deep granite gorge through the rolling, verdant hills of Limousin and this gorge is surprisingly wild, heavily forested, with no bridges, houses or roads for the length of the run. The only sign of civilisation is the occasional glimpse, through the trees, of the main Paris to Toulouse railway line as it dives in and out of tunnels. The granite rock gorge makes this into a superb, feisty, continuous run which rarely drops below class 2, and one long rapid closely follows another. Big clumps of granite, outcrops, ledges, and individual boulders, all make for clearly defined eddies, shoots, and plenty of little play waves.

Description

Put in at the old bridge at **Vigeois** where there is a picnic site and car park on the right bank next to the Gite d'Etape (it is also possible to put in 500m upstream at the Pont du Jargassoux). It's probably worth taking 5 minutes to walk down the path on the river left to scout the weir and mill shoot which is 300m below the bridge. The weir is normally shot through the old mill shoot on the river left, class 2 water then follows with, moss covered rocky sides to the river, and dense, darkly-forested valley sides rising to the sky line. 300m downstream brings you to a little cliff on the right and a deep pool and eddy line ideal for tail squirts.

A series of long rapids with small play waves takes you down and around a sharp left hand bend - just "a long green whoosh". Then, look out for a single power cable over the river and a rock bluff island on the right - this marks the first class 3 rapid with a big wave, **'le Saut de Moine'** (the Monk's leap). Just below here *le Brezou* stream comes in from the left with another wave train rapid below. There's a well built masonry wall on the left supporting the railway line and then the river bends west and then south again, the sides narrow in, the gradient steepens, and a rock outcrop on the left marks the approach of the next class 3 rapid **'l'equerre'** (the set-square) - a small fall with a sharp turn left.

The river bends back to the railway line - marked by another wall, followed by another bouncy rapid with big rocks/outcrops in the middle of the river - this is probably best run right. The valley then widens out on the right and there's a short stretch of relatively flat water. A meadow on the right has a track to the hamlet of *Vaynas* that could offer emergency egress if needed.

There's a small island then the valley and river narrow and the good times roll again with a fine class 3 rapid and a big surf wave marking the start of **'le passage des Serpents'**- continuous rapid after rapid, culminating in *'le Gros Train'*.

After this things quieten down as the gorge widens out, the river bends round to the left, with a grassy field on the left popular with locals for picnics (and a possible alternative take out). High up on top of the hill on the right you can see the 12th century **Château de Comborn** and then a last couple of easy rapids lead you down to the bridge and the **take out** on the left bank upstream.

Don't be tempted to continue past here because downstream are the scenic Gorges du Saillant, blocked now by three high dams, hydro power stations, and sterile reservoirs. These can be viewed from a tourist viewpoint off the D9, signposted as the *'Site de la Roche'*. Good views, but a dearth of ice cream shops!

Vézère - Canoe Centre, weir and campsite at Uzerche.

Saillant to Montignac **51 km of class 1 (2)** **no stars**

The Vézère comes out of its gorge at Saillant and changes character completely - it now meanders slowly in a flat valley past the outskirts of the city of Brive with numerous weirs that require portaging - hence this is not a popular stretch.

Montignac to Limeuil **47 km of class 1** ★ ❁❁ ☺

Water quality - OK. Temp. - warm. 20 cumecs? Busy? <200

Summary

On this lower stretch of the river, the Vézère cuts a deep meandering valley through the limestone plateau of the Perigord Noir. This lower valley of the Vézère is a UNESCO World Heritage Site, famous for the numerous caves inhabited by pre-historic man, with famous cave paintings as exemplified by the Gottes des Lascoux. Consequently, the villages and roads are very busy with tourists, so it seems a good idea to explore the valley by canoe, with short expeditions by foot to the pre-historic sites.

Dave Hallewell writes 'This stretch is easy paddling through spectacular limestone gorges and overhangs. There are plenty of beaches making stopping easy and there are day hire canoes on the river for most of the time but it is never really crowded. There are frequent access and egress points at most bridge crossings with good road access along most of the river. **Les Eyzies** is a 'must stop' point for refreshments, to explore, and to view the rock house buildings - land on the left bank in the middle of the town at the foot of the town square'.

In terms of the paddling the valley is often described as being a smaller version of the Dordogne. Also like the lower Dordogne, the paddling is easy with a gentle current, bubbling riffles, and no weirs or other dangers. The most popular and scenic stretch of the river is between Montignac to Les Eyzies. There are several riverside campsites, but as we ourselves didn't paddle this section it's unfair to make recommendations. Note that this is a popular tourist area - prices reflect this and it is also probably a good idea to book your campsites in high season.

Avocet

International river classification of difficulty

Class 1: Easy
Fast moving water with riffles. Few or no obstacles.

Class 2: Moderate
Small rapids with regular waves. Some manoeuvring required but easy to navigate.

Class 3: Difficult
Rapids with irregular waves and hazards that need avoiding. More difficult manoeuvring required but routes are normally obvious. Scouting from the shore is occasionally necessary. Open canoes without a spraydeck risk swamping.

Class 4: Very difficult
Large rapids that require careful manoeuvring. Dangerous hazards. Scouting from the shore is often necessary and rescue is usually difficult. Kayakers should be able to roll. Only the most expert open canoeist with a spraydeck would attempt this level. In the event of a mishap there is significant risk of loss, damage and/or injury.

Class 5: Extremely difficult
Long and very violent rapids with severe hazards. Continuous, powerful, confused water makes route-finding difficult and scouting from the shore is essential. Precise manoeuvring is critical. Rescue is very difficult or impossible and in the event of a mishap there is a significant hazard to life.

Class 6: Nearly impossible
Difficulties of class 5 carried to the extreme of navigability. Might possibly be run by a team of experts at the right water level, in the right conditions, with all possible safety precautions, but still with considerable hazard to life.

Alan has assured Anne that the river was ideal for a family canoe trip - unfortunately Anne had failed to trust her instincts ......

French glossary

Robin and Paul go canoeing

ENGLISH	FRENCH
Bank (river)	rive
Bouyancy	flottabilite
Bouyancy aid	gilet (de securité)
Bouyancy bag	gonfle
Breakout	stop
Bridge	pont
Canoe	canoe
Capsize	chavirer
Capsize & swim	désaler
Cliff	falaise
Confluence	confluence
Current	courant
Downstream	en aval
Drop (1-2m)	seuil
Drop (3m+)	chute
Eddy	contre
Eddy-line	port-feuille
Ferry or shuttle	navette
First aid	premiers secour
Flow	débit
Follow	suivre
Footbridge	passerelle
Gauge	échelle
Gorge	gorge
Gradient	dénivelée
Hole	trou
Hole [sic]	trou
Karabiner	monsqueton
Kayak	kayak
Left	gauche
Level	niveau
Loop	soleil
Metal stake	ferail
Mushroom (sic)	champignon
Navigable	navigable
Paddle	naviguer
Paddle (noun)	pagaie
Path	chemin, sentier.
Play-hole	trou à chandelles
Pop-out	chandelle
Portage	portage
Pour-over	pleureur*
Put-in	point d'embarquement
Raft	raft
Railway	chemin de fer
Rain	pluie
Rapid	rapide
Ravine	ravin, canyon
Reverse	marche arrière
Right	droite
River	rivière
Road	route
Rock	rocher
Rock or boulder	caillou
Roll (verb)	esquimoter
Rolling wave /small stopper	rouleau*
Section (of river) or gap	passage
Shoot (a rapid)	sauter
Spate	crue
Spraydeck	Jupe or Jupette
Stopper	rappel
Support stroke	appui
Swim	nager
Syphon	syphon
Take-out	point de débarquement
Throw line	corde de securité
Tow back	rappel
Tree	arbre
Tributary	affluent
Undercut	drossage
Un-runnable	infran (chissable)
Upstream	en amont
Volume	volume
Waterfall)	cascade
Weir	barrage

FRENCH	ENGLISH
Appui	support stroke
Avant	before
Baigner, nager	swim
Caillou	rock or boulder
Cascade	waterfall
Champignon	mushroom [sic]
Chute	drop (3m+)
Contre	eddy
Droite	right
Drossage*	water sliding sideways towards or under a cliff found typically on bends.
En amont	upstream
En aval	downstream
Esquimoter	roll (verb)
Falaise	cliff
Gauche	left
Giclé*	literally spurt, or the last stroke
Incidence	used with gauche & droite means pointing left or right
Infranch-issable	un-runnable

FRENCH	ENGLISH
Marche	reverse
Navette	ferry or shuttle
Naviguer	paddle
Pagaie	paddle (noun)
Pagaille	big mess (almost swearing)
Passage	section (of river) or gap
Passerelle	footbridge
Planiol	flat water (boring)
Pleureur*	pour-over
Port-feuille	eddy-line
Rappel	stopper
Rive	bank (of a river) = Ha Ha
Rocher	rock
Rouleau*	small stopper
Sauter	to shoot
Seuil	drop (1-2m)
Stop	breakout (verb and noun)
Sous	under or below
Suivere	follow
Trou	hole [sic]
Vague	wave
Veine	green tongue

Common expressions used by ordinary folk in their day-to-day lives:

ENGLISH	FRENCH	ENGLISH	FRENCH
Hi	Salut	Car	bagnole
Bye	Ciao	Purloin	squatter*
Mate (male)	copain	Pinch	piquer*
Mate (female)	copinne	Gang or boys	les gars
Cute	chouette	Stupid or stupid git	con ***
Thing	truc	Face	guelle**
What's his name	machin	Shut your face	ta guelle! ***
A sort of	un espèce de	Unwound	decontracté
Bloke	mec	Relaxed	relaxe
Geezer	type *	[Sic]	cool
Company	boite	[Sic]	stressé
Joke	blague	Awful (tricky one)	pas terrible
Grub	bouffe*	Shitty, awkward	merdique **
Eat	bouffer*	Naff	nul*

** star ratings indicate inadvisability of use in polite society, though it must be remembered that the French do swear considerably more than the British.

Now try this little extract and see how you get on -

"Oh, salut les gars. J'ai fait la navette jusqu'a la passerelle en amont de l'infran et putain! Il y a un passage bien merdique dans la gorge. J'ai parlé au mec de la boite de rafting qui m'a dit qu'il faut faire un stop dans la contre derrière un grande caillou près de la falaise, puis passer la chute avec incidence gauche pour rester a gauche parçe qu'a droite il y a un espèce de syphon. Si je tombe dans le rappel je sais que je ne pourrai pas esquimoter et j'ai pas envie de nager la-dedans"

"Sans blague? Decontracte toi! Reste cool! Je l'ai fait l'année dernière avec machin de Sisteron et c'est chouette, tu saute le truc avec un bon giclé droite et c'est tout. Allez! Viens bouffer avant qu'on cherche la bagnole"

Good luck and Bon voyage, Robin Knapp.

Glossary of river terms

Boulder garden - big rocks tastefully positioned in a rapid to give pleasure to boaters.

Breakout - an 'eddy' that a boat can use to break out of the current and then to stop in.

Camera vulture - avaricious bird with a large black beak that hovers below rapids.

Canoe - an open or Canadian style canoe. Note for American readers: Europeans often use 'canoe' as a generic name for all types of canoes and kayaks.

Chicken shoot - an easier way down a rapid that by-passes the main action.

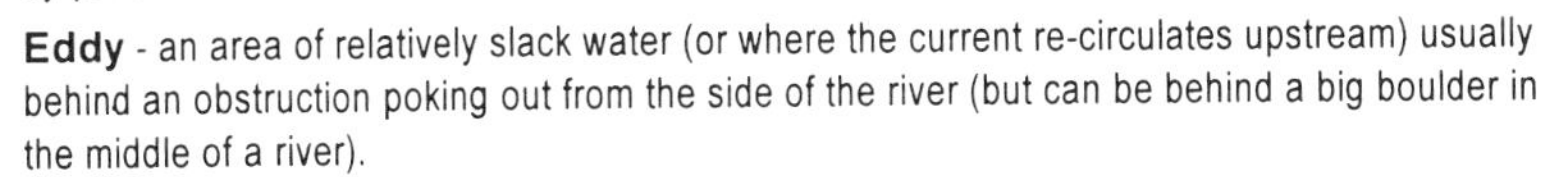

Eddy - an area of relatively slack water (or where the current re-circulates upstream) usually behind an obstruction poking out from the side of the river (but can be behind a big boulder in the middle of a river).

Eddy-line - the transition line between the main current and the slower calmer water of the eddy. Best crossed at speed!

Glissiére - a canoe chute built down the face or side of a weir and designed so that in normal water conditions you can shoot the weir in relative safety without getting out of your boat - exhilarating!

Hole - normally formed on the downstream side of a rock or similar underwater obstruction. There is usually a 'stopper' on the downstream side of the hole. Individual holes can be playful, tempting, humiliating, or downright dangerous.

Hot Dog - French term for an inflatable canoe, holding one or two persons that can be propelled with single of double paddles. These are a lot of fun for beginners and also used by experts for some extreme first descents. Americans call these 'Duckies'.

Kayak - small boat shaped like a banana, with a hole in the bottom from which the occupant hangs. Can be propelled the wrong way up by experts.

Kayaker - extreme form of deviant paddler (semi-human): uses a double ended paddle. Often called 'river maggots' by rafters because of their habit of infesting holes on a river. Canoeists and paddle rafters reckon that kayakers 'have twice the paddle but half the brains'.

Paddle - length of wood or plastic/metal: people hold one end and dip the other end in water to achieve a dramatic personality change.

Paddler - deviant form of human

Pin - where a boat is held by the current against a rock or other obstruction. May be vertical or horizontal, and underwater. Usually a serious incident and may be life-threatening.

Play Boater someone who changes their boat more than twice a year, each time for something shorter, in the hope that it will make them a better paddler.

Play spot - section of water used by over-grown children for water play with rubber and plastic toys. Those playing should beware the enticements of 'camera vultures'.

Portage - favourite activity of older canoeists. Wise boaters portage when in doubt.

Pour-over - the current pours over the top of a rock and then drops vertically, usually into an evil hole. Hard to see from upstream until it's too late, so potentially dangerous.

Put-in - start of excuses and commencement of a river trip.

Raft - inflatable boat used for descending white water rivers: appeals to those with a rubber fetish. Referred to by other paddlers as 'rubber bus', 'cattle wagon', 'pig boat', 'river barge', etc.

Roll - short for 'Eskimo roll'.

Scout - the act of inspecting a rapid or difficult stretch of river: 'When in doubt: get out and scout'. Exercise for eye muscles and imaginative excuses.

Sit on Top - 'Normal' kayaks or canoes have a big hole in the top (the cockpit) in which the occupant sits. If you capsize the water flows in this hole and fills the canoe up so it becomes very heavy and is hard to rescue and empty. It is also very difficult to climb back in again when swamped. A 'sit on top' is a sealed kayak/canoe with a depression in the top (instead of the cockpit) where the paddler sits. For the beginner, these boats have lots of advantages.

Stopper (British) / Reversal (American) / Hydraulic jump (Engineering) - a breaking wave on the downstream side of a hole that re-circulates like a window blind rolling itself up: bad ones will do this to you!

Surf - kayaks, rafts, canoes, etc. can surf a river wave just like people ride ocean waves.

Take-out - finish point of a river trip - usually followed by ice creams and lies.

Subscribers

Appendix D

Thank you to the following who helped launch this book by subscribing prior to publication:

Mike Adams
Crispin Agar
Linda Allin
David Andrew
Phil Arnold
Jen Ash
Marion Barnacle
A C Beecroft
Pooh Bear
Jevan Berrange
Phil Blain
Graham Bland
Black Blakeney
Chris Bonnington
Martin Burgoyne
Mike Chambers
Brian Churchill
M Clark
Andy Cole
Helen Cole
Peter Collins
Mick Coyne
R Cox
Phil Dean
Colin Eades
Colin Eastwick
Lee Emmett
Chris Fothergill
J W K Fraser
Ed Gertler
Andy Hall
Rob Hastings
Pete Hennessy
Mike Hewlett
Helen Holgate
Dave Horrocks
Roger Huyton
J H Kay
Dan Knowles
W Lebroy
G S Lelliot
Derek Livingstone
John Lovell
Roy Mackenzie
Nick McDonald
Carol Midwood
Allen Miller
Richard Munday
Iain Penketh
J Pinkerton
Ross Purdy
Nigel Ragg
Chris Randall
Bill Ransom
Milly Reid
David Ross
Louise Royle
Frank Ryan
Ian Seed
John Sellers
J P Shaw
Ian Sherrington
David Simpson
John Sole
Duncan Stirling
Lester Stuart
Mike Sunderland
Chris Taylor
Peter Taylor
Alan Tilling
Stuart Wagstaff
John Watson
H A E Wilkins
Tim Wheeler
D Wood
T S Wood

WHITE WATER SUMMER

Kayak & Rafting

Have fun and adventure next summer paddling the mild and wild Alpine rivers of France. We cater for all levels of experience (including total novice) and even cater for entire families. Intensive courses and leisurely holidays are available. Just call us for more details - go on - take the plunge !

Contact

Canoe Control mild and wild

The premier Professional British Alpine White Water School

Tel 01392 677167

email:stuart@canoecontrol.com

www.canoecontrol.com

ENDLESS RIVER

MAIL ORDER SPECIALISTS

01905 640003

Please contact us for your free colour brochure. Check our web site for monthly specials.

PO BOX 699, WORCESTER, WR2 6ZL

TEL/FAX 01905 640003

E-MAIL SALES@ENDLESSRIVER.CO.UK

WWW.ENDLESSRIVER.CO.UK

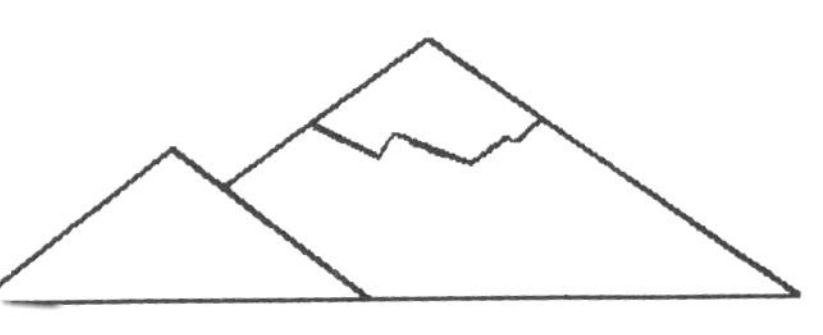

Four Seasons

Canoe – Kayak - White Water Rafting

Outfitter -Training Courses
Beginners to Advanced

Full range of Demo Boats to try on
Our small lake or the White Water Course

BCU Approved – AAA Licensed

Teesside White Water Centre
Tees Barrage
Stockton on Tees
TS18 2QW
Tel 01642 678000
E mail kanu@4seasons.co.uk
www 4seasons.co.uk

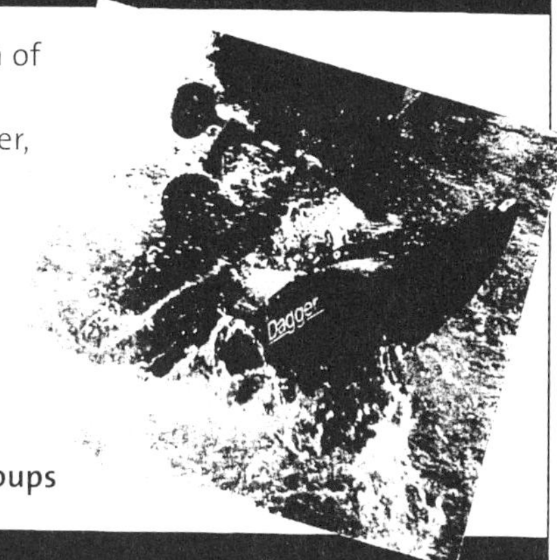

Dagger

January 1989 £1.20
Canoeist
Britain's most popular canoeing magazine
New generation helmets
Win an Ardèche holiday
An excuse to stay longer on the Ardeche
CANOEIST January 2001
33

Domaine de l'Astic

17th Century renovated stone farmhouse with swimming pool

Spacious self-catering accommodation and B&B
Ideal for families or groups

Only 10 minutes from the Ardeche River and Gorges

Janik and Graham Murphy
07150 VAGNAS
☎ 00 33 (0)4 75 88 10 88
www.domaine-lastic.fr
janik@domaine-lastic.fr

SNOWCARD TRAVEL & ACTIVITY INSURANCE

TAILOR-MADE SOLUTIONS FOR ACTIVE TRAVELLERS

Specialists in mountain sports activity travel insurance including white water rafting and kayaking.

Flexible cover options – medical and rescue only to full travel packages including equipment for single trips or annual multi trip policies.

Underwritten by specialist travel insurers and provided by General Insurance Standards Council members.

MEMBER
General Insurance
STANDARDS COUNCIL

Snowcard Insurance Services Limited are members of the General Insurance Standards Council

01327 262805 www.snowcard.co.uk